Sankat Mochan

Ashish Pandya

Preface

Historically, humankind has been subjected to numerous challenges that they have not encountered in the past. Ironically, these challenges propel them into a new trajectory, enabling them to explore the unchartered universe. This social phenomenon is equally applicable to each one of us, on a personal level.

At some point in life, every individual goes through a crisis they are least prepared for.

By the time we realize it, our entire belief system comes crashing down like a pack of cards. The dreams begin turning into a nightmare, and at every step, we are caught off-guard and unaware. The universe, as a whole, seems to be conspiring against us, and we end up feeling clueless.

In an instant, we do what we have always been conditioned to – blame everyone, but ourselves,
may it be a rival or different circumstances. However, if nothing works, we tend to blame destiny or karma. Nevertheless, the sufferings that follow remain inevitable and personal.

The questions within, continually running on a constant loop;

"Why me?"

"What have I done wrong?"

The next delusion occurs while trying to seek solutions externally. This could either include the help received from near and dear ones, or just an endless wait for favourable conditions to emerge. In the end, if nothing works, then we turn to God as a last resort.

Sometimes, I wonder if we earnestly worship God out of sheer joy and the connection we share with Him or merely trade with him, by desiring favour over worship.

The fact checks are paradoxical.

Let's seriously look at the life stories of such gods across religions. The most common denominator remains constant – the amount of suffering each one of them went through in their lifetime is far beyond human thresholds. So, the question arises; if they could not change their destiny, how could they possibly solve our issues?

The answer is simple.

The gods must not be treated as God, just because they are believed to possess special powers, but for the sheer humility they exhibited under the most challenging situations. They must not be worshipped because we have been conditioned to do so. Instead, due to their unwavering faith against all adversities, especially while adhering to the path of universal truth and principles. In a nutshell, God is the unique and superior being who led by example across constraints of human boundaries, and achieved the pinnacle of existence.

Faith makes it easy to be convinced, while logic finds it difficult to comprehend.

Are these values and principles manifested in our ancient and age-old scriptures still relevant today? Or do we merely recite them as rituals, to consider ourselves "religious"?
Do I worship God, for he is an exceptional occurrence in history? Or do I bow down to him, while shrugging off my duties?

This story is an outcome of such random thoughts that have continually bothered me, over the years. I am not sure how good or bad the result is, but I am convinced that we have not been left as orphans in this universe, during adverse situations. If we can have faith in these universal principles and implement them in real-life situations, then nature is bound to reciprocate positively.

All our prayers and questions do get answered. The only exception – they may not be at the time we want, or in the form we want them to be.

If this story generates faith and positivity even in one individual, I believe the work was worth all the efforts.

Thank you!

Chapter 1

"Hey, Raghav," screamed Lucky.

All heads turned towards Lucky, whose shout resonated through the modest ambiance of Syntel DataCorp's cafeteria. In contrast to the monotonous, modular office spread across five floors, the tiny room had a completely different appeal.

It generously provided its occupants with a much-needed break.

The setting was strikingly asymmetric, characterized by several lounge sofas and bean bags placed randomly between bright yellow dining tables and green chairs. A large mural leading up to the serving counter resembled a contemporary art décor, made of square glass pieces of varying sizes. The glass fragments were colored in bright pastel hues, with interesting and witty quotes engraved on them.

These intricacies greatly added to the setting's contrast.

Lucky, carefree, as always, was nonchalant to the whole attention. He began jumping and waving his hands at Raghav, who was waiting for his turn at the counter. Slightly embarrassed, Raghav stepped away from the queue and rushed towards Lucky, who was now seated with a bunch of colleagues.

"The HR Head is looking for you, and wants to meet you urgently! You need to hurry and meet him, man." Lucky gushed in a single breath, setting his impatience free.

"Looks like we need a party, bro," said Alok, whose satiric smile was not real enough to hide his jealousy.

"Man, you've already been promoted twice in the last two years, along with an 'Employee of the Year' award as a cherry on the cake. Yet, more good news awaits you, said Nitin, genuinely praising Raghav, "At least save some recognition for us poor men, my lord," he continued with a witty smile.

Being a man of few words, Raghav politely responded with a gentle smile.

He looked away as his unfazed eyes gazed intensely towards the glittering clouds. He wondered how many million miles the rays must have traveled before creating a thin silver line and eventually purging into obscurity.

Raghav had just turned twenty-seven a month ago, but in terms of life experiences, he had lived about twice his age. For a fortunate few, life ages like a fine wine – nurtured in a safe cellar, brewing and developing its exquisite taste gradually, and steadily. But, for the rest, life was equivalent to raindrops that fell without distinct direction or protection, where some drops become one with the earth's grime, and the rest flowed into the drain. Only a chosen few are lucky enough to gently dwell on beautiful petals, glistening brightly like pearls.

As far as Raghav remembered, only a few years passed easily, like a day. Else, other difficult days seemed like they took years to pass.

Growing up in a small town like Anandi, in Maharashtra, tends to narrow your canvas by half before your hands could even adjust to holding the paintbrush. Educationalists aggressively emphasize the importance of studying in a vernacular institution, and how it is the key to one's development. However, reality hits hard when you enter the mainstream world, where the English language is the primary medium of instruction and interaction. The insignificant advantages of being educated in a vernacular medium school evaporate as quickly as water droplets on a heated pan. Invariably you become subject to cruel mockery and remarks, owing to your *desi* dialect, pronunciations, and mannerisms.

Raghav's middle-class family ran a grocery shop, and despite their financial hardships, he decided to pursue his education in Mumbai, after the tenth standard. He ensured that his fees were paid on time, by taking up odd jobs and giving tuitions, while residing in his Aunt's house.

While his affluent classmates worried about failing their exams and repeating a year, Raghav's worries were filled with the fear of missing a year due to the lack of funds.

Different uncertainties; equal fear. While coming to terms with such aspects, God sure seemed to be playing an equal game.

It's true, the practical lessons taught by an empty wallet and an empty stomach are more enriching than the syllabus taught by esteemed universities, across the world.

On the other hand, Raghav knew that how hard you hit the ground is not important. Instead, the beauty of life lies in how high you bounce back, after.

His determination and hard work paid off when Mr. Martin, the HR Head at Syntel Datacorp, declared Raghav the only candidate selected out of one hundred and twenty others, during college campus placements.

His words still echoed in Raghav's mind, "I am not sure how long your love affair would last. But, mark my words, Raghav, this job is going to be an affair of a lifetime!"

Chapter 2

The memories of his first day at work, were deeply engraved in Raghav's mind.

The commercial building housing Syntel DataCorp's headquarters was a magnificent crest of modern architecture. Covered with a light-green tint, the exterior reflected the busy commercial street. A thin, almost invisible cable suspended the massive canopy at the building's entrance. It was almost as if the awning was floating in the clear, blue sky.

Every inch of the triple-height entrance lobby was clad in white statuario marble, with metallic grey strips interleaved in a random pattern. An impressive artifact, a metal globe, fabricated with welded wire mesh was placed right in the middle of the foyer. Currencies of various countries dominating the world economy revolved around the globe in intersecting orbits

"Is it money that moves around the world? Or is it the other way around? The entire universe revolving around money?" thought Raghav, and then laughed at his monologue," Today, one more person is joining the madness. Congratulations!" He chuckled to himself.

The insanity of this place was infectious. Barely a month into his employment, Raghav had well-adjusted and organized himself according to all the unorganized requirements - the busy schedules, late-night workings, project meetings, client calls, MIS presentations, budget meetings! The list was endless.

He soon understood that the most important trait a senior looks for in his team member is neither talent and intelligence, or passion.

It all converged into a simple, three-word rule, 'Never say no!'

Chapter 3

Much to his colleague's envy, Raghav became the most trustworthy associate, who could calm every fiery situation, in no time. Thanks to his modest background, he remained perpetually grounded, with a very limited list of friends who matched his intellect and wavelength.

Lucky, albeit, was a surprising exception.

Averse to being addressed by his official name, Lakhbirsingh Sodhi, Lucky's character completely contrasted Raghav's. He was a typical Punjabi *Munda* with curly hair, fair complexion, and an unruly, bearded appearance. Impulsive, unpredictable, and restless as always, he was not afraid of calling a spade a spade, and inviting strict confrontations with his seniors.

He originated from a rich business-oriented family, primarily engaged in manufacturing automobile parts for major brands. As a result, enlisting himself into the lucrative family business was as normal as a fish learning to swim in the pond; an obvious choice.

However, he intuitively, signed up for a campus-acquired job opportunity, to dive into the ocean of activities, happening within large-scale organizations.

The catalytic effect created by bringing Lucky and Raghav's drastically different personalities together, on the same stage, is accredited to Jhanvi.

It all began when she was in pursuit of a skit, depicting a humorous take on regular office life. She was determined to create an original and authentic piece, borrowing real-life details and cues from individuals in the office. Meanwhile, she ensured steering clear of popular movie spoofs and television series.

Lucky was ready to play the lead role, provided he was fully convinced with the script. That's where Raghav entered the scene, surprising everyone with his impressive writing skills.

Their combined efforts and the marvelous play ended with an awestruck audience and a standing ovation. This experience started a new chapter in their lives – friendship!

True to her nature, Jhanvi was the smiley-arc joining two diametrically opposite dots and spreading positivity and happiness, as always. In addition to being a trained *Bharatnatyam* dancer, Jhanvi was startlingly an ardent follower of rock music, as well! Full of contradictions, she was also an avid blogger, focused on writing about contemporary fashion, while looking elegant adorning traditional Indian outfits.

Chapter 4

The HR department was on the ninth floor, directly opposite the cafeteria. It accommodated nearly thirty employees, who occupied linear work stations, next to individual cabins.

Also, for the sake of privacy, two little meeting rooms were located right opposite the entrance, on either side. These would ensure that candidates coming for an interview do not have to pass through the entire office.

Next to them, the General Manager HR and Administration's glass cabin overlooked the beautiful skyline through the crystal facade.

Mr. Martin's cabin was right at the end of a long passage, dividing the manager cabins and the workstations.

Contradictory to regular buzzing, noise, chatters, and lively discussions, the department seemed very hushed today. Raghav couldn't help but notice the whispers, the moment he stepped into the place. There were no usual greetings from smiling faces, and no casual pats on the shoulder. It was almost as if he had accidentally entered a condolence meeting!

Faintly apprehensive, Raghav finally reached the dead-end. Letting out a huge breath, he knocked on Mr. Martin's cabin door.

"Hi, Raghav, come in! I was waiting for you."

"Yes, sir. I was slightly occupied with wrapping up the final details of the Boston project."

Mr. Martin did not appear to be at his usual best. For someone who always looked cheerful and happy, even under pressing and difficult circumstances, he was evidently poignant.

He looked outside, watching the gloomy skyline. Clearing his throat, he then began the conversation.

"Raghav, you know, I was the one who noticed you during the campus interview. I was the one who recommended you for Houston Financial Project. They are our most valued clients, across the United States," He paused for a moment, and then continued, "You are one among the few talented associates, carefully chosen for this project. Raghav, your visa would have been here, any time now," Mr. Martin's words lingered in the uncomfortable air.

But life is a stupid game! Even in adverse conditions and against the best opposition, you manage to strategically score a century. But, on another day, you are out for a duck against the weakest opposition, in your home ground.

"The COVID-19 outbreak has ceased everything, particularly on the economic front. No one could imagine how a tiny virus, not even visible to the naked eye, was capable of kneeling the so-called 'superpower' of the world, to the ground. The economic equations are never going to be the same. We are lucky to have survived the most dreadful economic earthquake of the century, but, the aftershocks are far from over yet.

Countries across the world are locked down, while people lose their jobs and struggle with pay cuts. It's a horrifying scenario everywhere, especially when the light at the end of the tunnel seems so far away. To make things worse, the United States' government is really becoming aggressive over curbing the H1B visas. They are rapidly promoting local recruits, and are even ready to pay more. 70% of our market comprises American clients, and we just cannot afford to lose them.

The newly appointed CEO, Mr. Lokesh Raman, is an astute professional. He has come up with a single-minded focus on improving the profit. Also, considering his history and past decisions, he can go to a great extent to prove his point.

For instance, last week, we were provided with a clear mandate to slash the Human Resources cost by half. I tried dodging it for quite some time. However, today, his desk handed me the list."

Mr. Martin paused for a moment, and gulped down an entire glass of water. In a very low but firm voice, he started again, "Raghav, I am sorry, but you are one among the ones being laid off,"

The dreaded pause was back, "Effective immediately."

He then continued, "As per the policy, you will be entitled to 2 months' salary, and of course, a good recommendation letter. But I am afraid, beyond this, I cannot be of any help."

His employer's voice struck Raghav like a thunderbolt. Everything just went blank, before his eyes. A shiver down the spine, he almost felt paralyzed, unable to act, and unable to react. For a moment, he wished for this to be a nightmare. He prayed somebody would shake him out of bed.

Unfortunately, the impending reality was far more dreadful than a nightmare.

Gathering himself in bits and pieces, he tried voicing out, "But Sir, many projects are being implemented outside the United States. Is it not possible to fit into a single one of them? Besides, it's not the end of the road for the company! We have several projects in the pipeline, which would surely-commence sooner or later. It's just a matter of time! Why does it have to be so harsh!"

Otherwise very docile, Raghav was barely able to control his outburst.

Mr. Martin just shook his head in denial.

"Sir, for once, I may agree that the company's well-being and profits are the management's prime goal. But ironically, we, as employees, have never prioritized our health and gains while fulfilling the company's goals. How can our hard work, sincerity, and efforts worth so many years be merely ruled out because of a struggle that lasted for a couple of months? Is this fair?"

"Life is unfair, my dear. The truth is more bitter than poison. I am afraid, you are in no position to defend it."

He was trying his best to utilize his HR experiences to cool down Raghav.

"Although in person, I am in sync with your emotions, but sadly, the company doesn't run on emotions. At times, it's compelled to make decisions unjust from an individual perspective, but highly imperative for larger interests and longer horizons. The pawns are destined to be sacrificed, saving the king and the queens. The rules of chess used to legitimize these honor killings are given a beautiful name here. It's called the 'Corporate Strategy.'"

Raghav couldn't say a word.

He continued, "Mr. Raman is a ruthless man. I'll put my best foot forward and try to help you, but you need to accept the fact and come to terms with it as soon as possible. When a house catches fire, you don't have the luxury to cry. Try to save whatever you can. That's all I can say."

Also, please meet Shivani, my assistant, in the evening. She will guide you through the formalities. All the best!"

"Thanks, sir." Raghav said, "I am thankful for everything the company, and especially, you have done for me. Please don't get me wrong! I am not sarcastic. I would rather remember this place and all these people for hundreds of beautiful memories, than one bitter moment. Thanks." He resonated with his life's philosophy.

In a flash, he got up from the chair and dashed out of the cabin. He saw a few familiar faces staring at him, trying to analyze his expressions, his body language, and finding a rare opportunity to learn the practical aspect of a lesser-known subject of the HR curriculum –Retrenchment.

But right now, his mind was cluttered with so many ambiguous questions, making such observations a trivial matter.

Why on earth, had this happened to him?

Where did he go wrong?

Did he do something wrong?

What's next?

Is this the end of the road? Or just a very sharp turn that he needs to navigate through?

Whatever it was, he had to make a firm promise to himself that the unmapped road ahead was certainly going to haul some serious challenges with unknown twists and turns, towards him. He had no choice left, but to move on.

"We want that party, buddy," Vinay announced from his chair.

Raghav was still lost in his thoughts and didn't realize how he had crossed the entire corridor and entered the canteen on the opposite side.

"Here comes Mr. Raghav, the future NRI, or Non-Reliable Indian!" He joked, "Your visa must have arrived, and I know HR has called you for the same. When is the flight, dear? Let's celebrate!

"I truly owe you all a treat," Raghav responded.

"I am not sure if I would ever get a chance to offer you treat again. I want to thank everyone from the bottom of my heart for all the beautiful memories. I'll cherish them for the rest of my life. Today, the treat is on me. Please order whatever you like!" Only God knew where he got his strength from, as Raghav looked surprised by his own response.

"Oye, this sounds like a farewell speech!" Lucky yelled.

"Yes, dear, you guessed it right. I am not going to the United States. I am just going out of the company. It's a pink slip. Today is my last day here."

"Raghav, my friend, telling a lie is an art," Vinay added, "And you know you are nowhere close to it!"

"I wish it were a lie," Raghav was now looking at the floor, "I wish someone would pinch me out of this dream. A really dreadful dream."

He raised his face in determination, "It is time for a reality check, guys! The writing is on the wall, which is why HR called me in. Today is my last day with the company; with your company."

Lucky got up. He was fuming, "I am going to speak with management and make them answerable. They just cannot do this."

He then left, while Raghav went back to his desk and began packing up his things. When he woke up this morning, nothing could have prepared him for what the fateful day had in store. In just a few hours, he had lost his job, and all his dreams of making it big, suddenly started fading away. They seemed impossible to reach now. The formalities that followed were even more painful. Going from one department to another seeking clearance and reiterating the incident to everyone was bruising the wound deeper and deeper.

Chapter 5

Lower Parel railway station looked fairly overcrowded today. Descending from the foot-over bridge, Raghav observed the sea of faces flooding every square inch of platform number one. Different faces, but the same expressions. Each seemed unsure of why they were here, what they were doing, and where they were going. Everyone was trying to find their own space, and in the bargain, pushing others, while ultimately being pushed into the train. The train, running from one station to the other, throwing them on to their respective stations.

The rat race continues!

The railways have continued maintaining those huge, antique clocks, hanging from the platform roof, and manifesting a historical heritage, besides time. The clock displayed 7.30 PM. It took a while to realize that he was too early compared to his regular timing. He couldn't remember the last time he left the office before 9.30, at night. The indicator was flashing the next train's arrival. It was the 7.36 PM slow train to Borivali. The crowd began taking their positions with military discipline.

Completely disinterested, Raghav just dragged himself towards the first-class compartment. The train arrived, and he was pushed inside.

It's common knowledge that you don't have to try too hard to get inside a crowded local train. All you need to do is just place yourself near the entrance. The crowd completes the formality. The position inside is harsh and hilarious, at the same time.

One of your hands may pass over someone else's shoulder, trying to grip the handle. The other hand, meticulously handcuffed by the people surrounding you. It's impossible to figure out who is stamping your shoes, and whose face is buried in your chest. However, this is where the spirit of a true *Mumbaikar* gets manifested.

In all adversities, each face radiates in a Zen-like trance!

Raghav's thoughts were running faster than the train, crossing out one option after another, and eventually reaching nowhere. It was the train, in the end, that won the race. Although late by five minutes, it did reach its final destination, Borivali.

The confusion was getting chaotic.

He was not sure, how he would be able to communicate this news to his parents. Barely six months ago, he had a difficult time convincing them to move to Mumbai. They were happy and complacent, in their own world.

Despite being really poor in the field of drama, Raghav had to throw tantrums and shed some tears in order to bring them to the city.

However, the goalposts had reversed post-half-time, like in a game of football. Now, was the time to hide his real tears in their presence.

Just outside the station, near the vegetable market, Raghav saw a long queue for share-a-*rickshaw*. Normally, the 3-kilometer journey to his house would barely take fifteen minutes. But today, he wished it would stretch for hours.

Nothing seemed normal today. Since the traffic was moderate, his *rickshawala* began racing the roads, completing the ride in record time. He did not realize when the other two passengers got off. Raghav was still gazing outside, reluctant to get off until the *rickshawala* began asking for the fare.

"Sir, *dhandhe ka time hai, khoti mat karo*. Please hurry up. I need to complete ten more trips before I close for the day."

Still clueless, Raghav nodded his head and got off at the crossroads of his colony.

The colony housed around forty buildings, constructed by the housing development authority, catering to lower-income groups. Each four-story buildings, visibly identical in design and layout, were home to people hailing from different walks of life. The staircase located right in the center divided each floor into two parts with six apartments on either side. The common corridor leading to each apartment was at least six feet wide, and confined to a concrete parapet. The doors, made out of solid wood, had stood strong for at least 40 odd seasons of summers, winters, and the rains.

Well, all thanks to its seasoning process.

Technically, a raw wood has to undergo this transformation process, where it is subjected to rigorous drying and wetting, one after the other. This makes it strong and sturdy, ready to withstand the most severe storms.

Raghav was unaware of the technicality. However, not untouched by reality.

He looked at the doors, not for inspiration, but in anticipation. He wished none of them were open today. It was customary in such colonies, for doors to remain open throughout the day. All had free access to any house, any time, and any life. Privacy was neither a privilege, nor a prerogative, whether you liked it or not.

"So early, Raghav?"

Barely turning right towards his apartment on the second floor, he heard Asha *Tai's* voice from the first door.

"All is well?"

Unable to find the right answer, he managed to fake a smile in response.

"The struggle starts right here," He murmured in silence and quickly rushed towards his apartment located right at the end.

The doorbell was a seldom-used amenity. Just like the others, his door was open to welcome him, as well.

The layout of the room was straight and simple, beginning with the living room followed by a passage with the kitchen and bathroom on either side. The combined toilet was at the far end. The square-shaped window on the wall, adjacent to the door provided a good amount of natural ventilation. The floor covered with cement mosaic tiles imparted a pleasant, heritage look, while the walls painted off-white made the place appear spacious.

His father was seated on a sofa-cum-bed, completely engrossed in scrolling through the breaking news playing on the TV screen. Watching the news for an hour, every day, was now a part of his daily routine. Thanks to the TRP rat-(ing) race, where a celebrity sneezing is potentially breaking news, and real issues take up the remaining time slots.

He was completely unaware of his son's presence, and of the most heart-breaking news, he was about to announce. Raghav silently sat on the chair, took off his shoes, totally lost in thoughts, and tried to gather strength.

"Listen, is someone there at the door?" Meena *Tai* inquired from the kitchen.

Raghav jolted back to reality, hearing his mother's shout.

"It's me" His voice took a while to emerge.

"*Arey*, when did you come? I didn't realize it." Raghav's father turned off the TV, while his mother came out of the kitchen.

"You didn't call us before leaving? You're a little early today! I hope you are fine?" she handed her son a glass of water

Raghav took the glass and gulped it down in one go, trying to avoid her eyes.

Surprisingly, all mothers are blessed with an uncanny sixth sense. They can instantly identify when something is bothering their kids.

"Raghav, are you okay?" She asked, "Don't pressure yourself. We may not understand your work issues. But one thing we can surely advise is that you need to draw a line between your professional Life and personal Life. Once you are out of the office, leave those problems there. Your home is a place where you need to relax, and rejuvenate. If possible, try and take a break." His mother ran her fingers through his hair, with affection.

His eyes turned moist. It was time to declare the catastrophe.

"There is no need for a work-life balance from tomorrow," Raghav stated.

"What?" Raghav's father was confused by the statement he just made.

"I am not required to go to the office anymore," said Raghav.

"We are unable to understand what you are trying to say," his mother began to sense that an unfortunate incident had taken place.

"*Maa, Baba*, please listen carefully," Raghav was almost choking, "I have been sacked from my job."

His parents felt paralyzed, and unable to move.

"Trust me, and it's not my fault. If anything, it's the situation that needs to be blamed." Raghav began pouring out his heart.

"I'm not sure how life is going to be like from tomorrow, whether I'll get another job or not, or if I would be able to pay the home loan EMIs. I am definitely not sure if we could even manage our daily requirements. Life is too uncertain, too unpredictable, right now. We have read of such circumstances in books, and even seen them in movies. But, I never imagined it could happen to us one day, as well. After all, books and movies originate from real life, and it only takes a day to flip the entire life upside down."

Raghav's parents were too confused to even react. His father got up from the sofa, and came closer to him.

His mother was gently patting his back, "*Beta*, we don't have an answer to your problems, but rest assured we are with you through all of it. You may or may not find a solution right away, but I promise you, together, we can manage every situation. When life closes one door, it's surely going to open another!" Her voice turned more confident, "Even if it doesn't, we'll break the wall and create one!"

"If things happen as per our will, it's good. But if it doesn't, it's even better, because then it would be God's will. He will never let us down."

His father, a man of few words just like his son, could not express anything. He just came closer and hugged him tightly.

Tears began trickling down each eye, and sparkled as they merged.

His mother was the first to speak up, "Son, go ahead, take a warm bath, and come back. I have something tasty in store for you!"

His father nodded in acknowledgment, and encouraged his son to freshen up. Raghav's mother and made his favorite curry, and tried her best to cheer her son up.

They ate their dinner together, and soon, his parents retired for the night. Raghav decided to browse through his social media and email, before he went to bed.

That's when his phone lit up, with a message from Lucky, that read, 'Meet me tomorrow at Mysore Café @ 11 AM.'

Raghav was visibly confused because he had not seen Lucky for an entire day after he broke the news about being fired. Now, out of the blue, he received a message asking to meet.

Nevertheless, he decides to visit and find out what this was about.

Chapter 6

Café Mysore, running since 1940, was possibly one of the oldest food joints in Mumbai. Serving lip-smacking south Indian delicacies in a very simple, ethnic, decor, the café was a favorite among morning walkers as well as office goers, alike. Operating from six o'clock in the morning till eleven in the night, this place was swarming with patrons, barring only a few peaceful hours.

Eleven in the morning was one such time.

Lucky waved at Raghav from their usual corner table near the window. He had already ordered *Upma* for Raghav, a pineapple *sheera* for himself, and a filter coffee for Jhanvi. Yesterday, she was out of the office for a meeting, missing all that happened. Today, she desperately wanted to be with Raghav and had quietly sneaked out of the office for half an hour, under the pretext of bank work.

Along with the coffee, she also arrived on time. Looking a little nervous, she took a seat near Raghav, and held on to his hand. Jhanvi looked straight into his eyes with determination, and suddenly, he was prepared to face anything.

"I have put my papers down," Lucky was completely nonchalant in the announcement.

Jhanvi almost dropped her coffee, and Raghav was in complete denial, unable to accept any more shocking words.

"Come again? What are you saying? Are you insane?" Raghav couldn't control his feelings and his reactions.

"You are not working on the US project, then how did your name appear on the list of layoffs?" Jhanvi asked, surprised.

"Nobody has put me on the list. I have put the company on my 'blacklist,' and I don't want to put my efforts into a company with no human value, and no moral courtesy. We are just treated as parts of machines, and thrown out once worn out," said Lucky.

"But, isn't that the reality? We are indeed a part of a large mechanism. Even if we are working fine, and some part in the other corner doesn't perform well, the consequences are clear. We are bound to get stuck, and inevitably, be shut down." Jhanvi put forth a logical argument.

"There is a difference between men and machines, and the company needs to realize this. Whenever they earn a better profit, do they share it equally with the employees? Companies do not become great just by increasing their net worth. They become great by maintaining the highest standards of ethics, values, and principles, even during the most difficult times. Such companies boast of a glorious history of growth, over a hundred years," asserted Lucky.

"I wish I could do this!" Jhanvi was almost convinced by the argument, "But, I need to support my family. As you know, my father has retired and spent all his savings on my studies. I just can't let him down. I am sorry," she said.

"You need not. Your requirements are different, and mine is different," Lucky added.

Raghav quietly listened to Lucky's arguments. Although not fully convinced, he began, "Lucky, I can't win an argument with you, but for god's sake, don't do this! I am already sulking because of my issues, and I just can't bear the burden of you quitting, just for me."

"Hello!" Lucky immediately took the conversation's control back into his hands, "Don't consider yourself so important! For you, I wouldn't even buy this *Upma*! Everything here is being done only for one person, Mr. Lakhbirsingh Sodhi!"

For a while, the problem at hand took a back seat.

Lucky continued, "Anyway, the important point to meet up was not this. I wanted to discuss how we could quickly find ways to move forward. Raghav, you are going to get two months' salary, including other things like an accrued bonus, gratuity, and leave encashment. So, the timeline is fixed. You have exactly two months to get a new job, and we'll have to make every day of these sixty days count!"

Lucky continued, I have a few job consultants' references. They persistently kept calling me for openings I wasn't interested in. I am not sure if those positions are still open, but there's no harm in calling them back. So, immediately update your resume, and post it on multiple job portals. Make it more visible by refreshing it every few days. "

Raghav quickly interrupted his friend, "What about you? Why are you not trying? Sacrifice for a friend, hmm?"

Lucky reflectively said, "Let me admit it. This incident has changed my perception of people, and my perception of life completely. I am losing faith in the old saying, 'do good and good will happen to you.' I need some time to figure out my priorities, and whenever I decide on it, that will be the most important decision of my life. It's worth spending my time on, and for once, I feel fortunate to have that luxury. You guys continue, while I settle the bill."

They both just looked at each other. No words were exchanged.

Jhanvi, radiating positivity through every expression, said, "Things will be fine, so just stay cool, and have faith in yourself, alright?"

Raghav looked more composed, and reciprocated with a firm, confident smile.

Words are essential for communication. But for communion, silence is a prerequisite.

Chapter 7

The target was set.

Sixty days to go!

Raghav felt nostalgic, reminding him of his days in college. The reverse counting began on the day their examination dates were announced. That's when the discovery of books, notes, past papers, started simultaneously.

Alas, if only life would have been that simple!

The only rule here is that there are no rules! There are no books, no mentors, no past experiences. All questions are way beyond the prescribed syllabus. Premeditated answers had zero value, and he had to deal with those questions, just as they were.

One by one, and day after day.

Day-1:

"Hi. This is Raghav, here. I got your reference from my friend regarding a job opportunity in your firm. I'm assuming he was approached a couple of months ago. I just wish to know if the position is still open and if I could apply for the same?"

The plan was quite simple.

Raghav had prepared a list of HR consultants who approached Lucky, Jhanvi, and several other friends in recent months, and he was required to make at least eight to ten calls in a day.

A standard introduction, and a standard inquiry followed by atypical conversation. However, to his disappointment, the answers were standard, as well.

"The position was filled a long time ago."

"It's already closed. But, you can drop in your CV. We'll get back to you if a similar prospect opens up."

"IT is going through a lean phase due to the COVID-19 pandemic. We're unsure if it would pick up soon."

Every anxious minute took days to pass. While the days just passed by in minutes.

Day-15:

"It's another day, another fight." Raghav began motivating himself. He had made this his mantra, reciting it over a hundred times, each day.

Around 11 AM, he looked outside the window. The small bazaar near the main road's junction was buzzing with activities. Women surrounding vegetable vendors were busy honing their bargaining skills. The utility and medical shops were busy attending to a few customers. Life was pretty normal, outside.

But inside, it was anything, but normal.

He was tired of calling up job consultants. Now, it was time to approach other IT companies directly through their websites, or through other known references. Raghav's tasks for the day included sending his resume to at least ten such companies.

His mother, extremely caring over the past few days, brought him a cup of tea.

Suddenly, his cellphone rang. The screen flashed an unknown number. For a moment, his heart skipped a beat, and his pulse started racing faster.

"I really hope it's an interview call." He prayed. His mother also stopped for a minute.

"Is this Mr. Raghav?" A woman's voice spoke.

"Yes," He was visibly impatient, "May I know who's speaking?"

"Sir, I am calling from IDG Bank personal loan department. We provide loans at very attractive rates. Do you have any such requirements?"

Raghav was about to smash his cellphone on to the wall, but managed to control his emotions.

He was trying to be as polite as possible before his mother."

"Ma'am, my phone number is already in the do not disturb mode. How can you call me? Please don't compel me to file a complaint. Please, for god's sake, just remove my name from your list!"

"Please give me a minute, Sir. For people like you, working in the corporate sector, we have come up with an excellent scheme!" The lady was clearly not ready to take no for an answer.

Raghav's mother's presence acted as a firewall, preventing any unwanted content from coming out of his mouth.

He struggled to rephrase his words, "Ma'am, currently, I am unemployed. If your company still insists on offering a loan, then please go ahead. There is no guarantee that I would repay it. Is that fine?" He disconnected the call abruptly, almost fuming with anger.

Mothers, irrespective of their educational qualifications, are always more qualified than top B-school graduates, in terms of managing their kid's turmoil.

"The bathroom tap has been leaking since the past few days." She said, diverting his attention, "Raghav, can we call a plumber today?"

The shot fired in the air, accurately hit the bull's eye.

"Where do we get plumbers from? I don't know *Maa*; everyone is so unorganized here."

Raghav seemed to slowly fall into the trap, strategically placed by his adoring mother.

"You should enquire at the local hardware shop. They must know," she was prepared with a response.

"No one wants to improvise at all. Don't you think there ought to be better and improved systems in place?" Raghav continued, "Something like a common platform for such services, with a comprehensive list of respective technicians. So, whoever needs them, can readily approach them! Good for us, and good for them!"

Raghav was slightly surprised by his answer.

Suddenly, a vague idea began forming in his head. But, his mind was too cluttered to comprehend it.

"Okay, I'll go there, and find out."

He walked out of his room, towards the door. Slipping his feet into his sandals, he made sure that he took his wallet, and opened the door. The person, and the situation, you try to evade the most, is the one that usually confronts you first.

Mukesh was standing right in the middle of the corridor.

A short man with curly hair, and a dark complexion, Mukesh was always found wearing a pair of shorts and *baniyan*. He held the record of not sticking to one job for more than three months. The sole purpose of his existence revolved around keeping an eye on passers-by and peeping into everyone's life.

"Good morning, Raghav" His menacing smile disturbed Raghav.

"How is it that you are at home, at this time? Is the company closed? Or is it something else?" With a sarcastic look, he scanned Raghav from head to toe.

The society at large possessed a wicked norm. The good people paid the price for being good, while the cunning ones extract the price for being really cunning.

Raghav still had to learn the art of negotiating with such negativities. Slightly embarrassed, he just gave Mukesh a faint smile and hurriedly moved on to his short trip to the hardware store.

The shops were systematically lined up along the footpath, near the crossroad. Even without a prominent hoarding, one could easily identify the hardware store. It was stocked with different materials in every corner, covering every wall, every inch, and a small area of the footpath, as well.

"Material management at its best," Raghav wondered. There were a few customers waiting at the counter, and he waited patiently for his turn.

"*Bhai saab*, do you know any good plumber?" He inquired when it was finally his turn. "I have an urgent requirement."

The man on the counter was busy calculating the previous customer's bill. Without even looking at Raghav, he replied, "There is one, but he has not shown up today. God knows where he is! Give me your number. I'll pass it on to him if he calls back."

Raghav shook his head and thought, "Spare me the irony! Here I am, desperately looking for a job, and take a look at this guy. A job has come searching for him, and he is nowhere to be found."

"Is he not a regular here?" Raghav questioned.

"Actually, the work is not regular every day. So he may have skipped today or gone elsewhere," said the man, continuing his calculations, and not looking up once.

"This is so inefficient, and someone needs to streamline it. This can definitely be organized if someone decides to put in the efforts!" Raghav began wondering.

"But the question remains. Who is that person?"

Day 30:

"Lucky, this is going nowhere. Things are becoming really scary," Raghav said, on a video call with Lucky and Jhanvi.

Jhanvi was not at her usual best today, and looked upset even before Raghav expressed his alarming concerns. Still, she decided to put up a brave front. "What about your tele-interview the other day? Any reverts or call-backs?"

Raghav replied, "That's more of a back-end position, for maintaining an existing IT setup. I am not very keen on taking it up. But like they say, 'beggars can't be choosers.' I'll accept whatever comes my way, because I just can't bear this uncertainty anymore!"

"How about applying for an overseas firm? What if they have some requirements?" Lucky said

"Honestly, I will try anything and everything."

"Guys, there is one more bad news." Jhanvi said, and paused for a while, "I wish, I didn't have to share it during this point, but I guess, I don't have a choice. "

"Now what?" replied Raghav, "I hope you are safe?"

"Sort of," Jhanvi took a deep breath. Biting her nails, a nervous habit she had picked up on, she began, "I have been asked to relocate to Chennai. The client needs-site support. I need to fly tomorrow, and it may take me a year there, if not more."

"What the hell is this? I just can't believe all that is happening with us! Is this some kind of a cruel joke played by destiny?" Lucky almost broke his mobile screen.

Raghav was trying hard to hide his pain, an art he had been thoroughly practicing, over the last month.

"Nothing can ever go right with me. You move one step forward, and life pushes a thousand steps backward. Lucky, you are right. Life seems to have lost its sense of humor, and is playing stupid, sadistic jokes on us, one after the other!"

"And you know what?" We aren't even granted the luxury of crying!" He concluded with a knowing smile. "We can only laugh."

Three hearts shared the same pain, and expressed the same smile.

You are fortunate if you have friends to laugh with. But you are truly blessed if you have friends to cry with. The pale smile on their faces looked like a glorious, waving flag hoisted from the post of tears.

Day-59:

It was the final day of the countdown, a make or a break situation!

Raghav's interview with Accord Inc., was scheduled for 3 PM in their office at Bandra Kurla Complex, Mumbai's emerging commercial hub.

Completely drained by the last two months' struggle, he still needed to appear confident; he still needed to put on a brave face. Feeling at a loss through every fiber of his existence, he still had to convince the interviewer regarding his capabilities of generating profits for the company.

Raghav ate a quick meal and did a cursory check of his documents. He dressed up quickly, as he generally didn't require a lot of time to get ready.

"I should be back by at least 8.30, in the evening," He informed his mother, "But don't wait for me, and please have your dinner on time."

He touched her feet, "I desperately need your blessings today, *Maa*."

"They are always here for you," she gently ruffled his hair, "You may find this strange, Raghav, but I have a feeling that something good is about to happen. Let's pray for the best, *Beta*."

He reached the firm fifteen minutes before time, informed the HR coordinator, and patiently waited at the reception. The general ambiance appeared quite amicable. Employees walking around looked relaxed, and Raghav began comparing the new place with Syntel.

It was an immediate benchmark for him.

For reasons unknown, he still felt a strong connection with his previous company, and strangely, he never tried to shrug it off.

Shefali, the HR coordinator, informed him that an external audit was taking place, and things were not on the schedule. He would have to wait for his turn.

The interview began with the technical round, which started at 5 PM. Raghav had no trouble clearing it. The HR round took another hour, and he completed it without a problem.

He was amazed, and felt a lot more confident than before. The final round was supposed to be with the reporting manager.

The wait was getting longer, and the coordinator kept appearing every hour, just to inform him to, "Wait for another hour."

"The wait already stretched for over two months now. No harm in waiting for a couple more hours," He had to constantly keep motivating himself.

Raghav looked at his watch, which displayed 10.30 PM. Finally, Mr. Kuldeep, the reporting manager, arrived.

"I am so sorry, gentleman, the external auditor, took a lot of our time and brains. I am afraid I may not have anything left in here," he said, pointing towards his brain.

Raghav just smiled, while the reporting manager invited him inside his cabin. They took their respective seats, and Raghav appeared as confident as possible.

Mr. Kuldeep began, "Since you are meeting me, I reckon, you have cleared both the technical and HR rounds. But let me be honest, I don't give any leverage over these things, because nothing succeeds like success. You just need to be smarter than the technical guys. As a manager, we don't need to do all the legwork on our own. What do you think?"

Raghav was caught on the wrong foot. He began cautiously, "Sir, you may be right. But, I believe technical knowledge is the basic foundation on which a house is built."

"Oh, yeah," Mr. Kuldeep pierced straight through his eyes, and words, "No considerations, straight contradiction."

"Let me ask you a simple question. Syntel probably has the best standard operating procedures (SOPs), quality systems, data analytics, and a lot more. Given the opportunity, would you not share all the documents with us? Why should we waste additional time and resources devising the same?"

Raghav knew the game was over. The words came to him like a final whistle blow, just when he was about to score the winning goal.

"I am sorry, Sir, but that's unethical. I won't do that," Raghav's ethics preceded his ordeal.

"Then let me be blunt about it, as well," Mr. Kuldeep pressed the uncertain interviewee's pain point. "Raghav, I know you were fired from Syntel. Your CV says you've done exceedingly well throughout. So, just to compensate for a few bad months of business, your hard work worth several years were sacrificed in minutes! Now tell me, where were their ethics?" He said, without a blink of an eye.

When he didn't receive an answer, he continued, "Life doesn't work on ideology. You need to be smart enough to define ethics, based on the situation, and not by books. I'm sorry, but I do not hire 'bookish' people. I need smart people."

"You may be right, Sir. But, I believe I am not wrong," Raghav asserted his perspective. He was unshakeable, and said, "What the company did was according to their standards. I, on the other hand, believe in my values."

"I have nothing to say. Thank you, and goodbye, gentleman." Mr. Kuldeep said, and concluded their conversation.

Once again, Raghav's moral value defeated the material value. However, the reverse was the need of the hour. He was so near, but so far.

A defeat, after all, is a defeat. You could not gain extra time once the match was lost.

Raghav didn't know what to do next. He was completely numb and dumbstruck. He just walked and walked, directionless. Bandra railway station was at least 4 kilometers away, but he didn't intend to hire a cab. The countdown ended the next day with no offer in hand. He was just dragging himself, and dragging his thoughts along.

Chapter 8

He looked at the indicator, whichshowed1.15 AM.

"Oh, god!" He looked at his watch in complete disbelief. It was indeed, 1.15. He quickly took out his cell phone, which was in silent mode since three in the afternoon. He pulled down his screen's notification panel, and saw40 missed calls. He was certain that his mother, Lucky, and his father, everyone must have tried calling him several times.

He was about to call his mother, when a train entered the platform. It was possibly one of the last trains for the night. He entered the first-class compartment, and put the 3-months season ticket to use for one last time. The seats were all empty, and it took him a while to choose the preferred window seat. Raghav knew that too many options, at times, create more confusion than comfort.

He instantly dialed his mother's number.

"*Maa*," That's all he could muster.

"Raghav, where the hell are you?" She shouted from the other end.

"How could you be so irresponsible? We have been trying to frantically reach you for the last four hours, and you just didn't pick up the phone. Can you even imagine what we must have gone through?

"*Maa*, listen. I am so sorry. The phone was in silent mode," Raghav tried to compose her.

However, his mother was inconsolable, "Now, you listen carefully. I don't care about your job, your future. To hell with everything! We are leaving this place and going back to our town. I am afraid, and I don't want you to take any extreme steps!"

"Just stop it, *Maa*. I admit I am depressed. But not so depressed that I would consider committing suicide!" Raghav was about to set his anger free, but was distracted upon hearing a loud thump, instead.

Somebody had jumped into the running train.

The powerful beam of light, flashing from another train, blinded him for a second. He tried to open his eyes slowly. What he saw next was something straight out of a mythological fantasy.

Piercing through the light, there emerged a huge, masculine figure. His long, curly hair was covered by a golden crown, embedded with rubies and diamonds. The long, curvy ears lobes, stretched down further with oval earrings. The white *janoi*, running diagonally across his athletic chest, shone like a bright ornament. The strong, round biceps, carrying a golden mace in hand, could intimidate any stranger. The saffron dhoti, neatly tied around his waist, was complimenting his abs. Something waved at Raghav behind his back, which he couldn't figure out at that instance.

The 'figure' walked up to him. The face was of a monkey, and yet, very charming.

"Uhm, are you, Lord Hanuman?" Raghav stood in disbelief. Adjusting his tail, the 'figure' sat on the seat opposite Raghav, and closed his eyes, diving deep into meditation.

"Are you there, Raghav? Why are you not speaking?" Raghav's mother continued talking, as her voice reverbed through the cell phone, in the still of the night.

Raghav used this to divert his attention.

"There was some disturbance. I am listening, continue, what did you say?" he tried to distract himself, but couldn't help but stare at the 'figure.' "We should return to our hometown? *Maa*, at least you don't give up on me. I need you to support me!" he exclaimed desperately.

"*Maa*, I know that I am depressed, and clueless, and that I don't have any answer to any of the problems I am facing, or the pain I am experiencing. Moreover, I don't even understand, why would something like this happen to me? I have never wronged anyone. In fact, I've only helped all those I could. Then why is there nobody to help me? Can you tell me why, *Maa*?" Raghav questioned furiously.

"I know why!" the 'figure,' still meditating, exclaimed.

"I'm sorry?" Raghav asked, clueless.

"*Maa*, we'll discuss this once I am home. Should reach in an hour, don't worry. Bye," a dazed Raghav, ended the call.

He then started looking at the 'figure,' who was still was in deep meditation.

"Excuse me! You said something?" Raghav asked curiously

"Yes. I said, I have the answer to your problem," the 'figure' replied.

Raghav was now restless. "May I know who are you, and why are you in this get-up? That too, right now? Raghav asked, unable to control himself.

"Are you looking for trivial answers or enlightenment on things bothering you? Don't you think that all throughout life, we only waste our time on trivial questions, while missing out on understanding the real essence of our existence? That's the real reason for our misery," his prophetic words hit Raghav.

He continued, "I am Hanuman!" and paused for a moment, staring into Raghav's eyes, "I mean, I am playing Hanuman in *Ram-Leela* at Dadar Municipal ground. The show started late due to some technical difficulties, and I missed the last train from Dadar. So, I took up a taxi and rushed to Bandra, before I missed it there too. And I guess you are intelligent enough to figure that there was no time for me to change my costume, convincing enough?" he stopped, smiling at Raghav. His nose and lips were red—his smile, mischievous, yet pure.

Raghav, although not fully convinced, was more interested in knowing the other answers. "That's okay, but you were saying something about me and my problems," he said inquisitively, looking for answers.

"You are having a hard time in life. Am I right, or am I right?" he replied wittily.

"I am not good at pursuing my emotions, and anybody can decipher how I am feeling by looking at my face. It's no big deal!" Raghav answered prudently, continuing, "I am more interested in knowing the 'why' part. Why me? Why on Earth, am I going through this? What wrong have I done to suffer this way?"

"Your answer lies in answer to my question, my friend!" Hanuman exclaimed. "Do you think you are the first person on Earth to suffer?" Hanuman asked as Raghav denied, shaking his head sideways.

"Then, are you the last one?" Hanuman asked as Raghav denied again.

"No, right?" Hanuman

"But that doesn't reduce my suffering, does it?" Raghav, unconvinced, asked. "My pain is still pain. It can't disappear just by knowing others hurt too! The question is still unanswered."

"You can give suffering any name. Call it *Karma*, or sin, or anything, doesn't matter. The problem lies with our perception. Our mind is conditioned to categorize things into two parts, 'good' and 'bad.' Anything which doesn't bother me, or stress me out, is always good and welcome. Whatever troubles me, or puts me out of comfort, is bad and a big no-no. But remember, the bad time is a great teacher, the best, in fact. The most valuable lessons of life are learned in the most difficult times. You can only achieve when you step outside of your comfort zone." he was making sense to Raghav now.

"Let me give you an example," Hanuman continued, "a little bird, barely able to walk on its feet, hesitates to move on the branch where it is nested. How do its parents make it take their first flight of faith in this endless sky?" his question was followed by a pause, as Raghav's curiosity grew

"Simple, they just throw it in the air!" Hanuman's answer surprised Raghav, as he continued, "And it is only at this point, that the little bird realizes the strength of its wings. The gust of wind supporting it from beneath its wings, sets it free. This free bird now touches the clouds, talks to rainbows, and dares to look beyond the horizons. So, what do you think was good for the bird? A comfortable nest on the familiar branch or the flight of fantasy in the sky?"

It calmed Raghav, but didn't satisfy him. For once, Raghav found some solace in his sufferings. But the logical mind still asked for more.

"Such stories are good to read in books, but real life treads on uncertainties, and that uncertainty is the real killer." Raghav asserted.

"Like science, life also works on some definite principles," Hanuman replied as the discussion shifted to science.

"What is gravity?" Hanuman questioned. "Simply put, it is the force that keeps you grounded to Earth. When you lift your leg up, you don't even realize that it's the gravity that brings it down, enabling you to walk. At the same, if you wish to jump from a height, the same gravity also breaks your bones. Can you blame gravity for this? No! In the end, it bottles down to your choice! In either of the cases, the nature of gravity remains unchanged. It is because you chose to stay ignorant, that you suffered. Like gravity, 'uncertainty,' too, is an essential part of life! How dull would this life be, if we knew everything that was to happen, every time! The TRPs of a game's highlights would always be less than the real games. If, uncertainty causes fear and confusion, it is the same uncertainty that keeps you excited, and motivated. It is a universal law, and doesn't change as you please!"

It made sense to Raghav, but he wouldn't say it and kept arguing instead. "But why did God create suffering at all? Was it really required?" He could have planned something better and more utopian."

"Have you read Ramayana?" Hanuman, traversing across psychology and science, came to his forte. "Everyone knows Ramayana is our holy book, and signifies the glory of Lord Ram. It narrates the story of Lord Ram's exile from Ayodhya to keep his father's oath, which is followed by the abduction of his wife Sita, and which ultimately ends with the killing of evil Ravana. 'The victory of good over evil.'"

"Even kids know this. But this is where the problem lies! We've always treated it as just a story, a sacred book, or, at most, a holy scripture. Idolising Ram as 'Lord' Ram, without imbibing his essence, is probably the biggest injustice we do to him. The suffering, the pain, the struggle that he has gone through is conveniently covered up in the colors of flowers offered at his feet. The values, the principles, the high ethical standards, he exhibited in all adversities, are all shrunk to *bhajans* that we sing for him.

You need to envisage his situation from a human perspective. Imagine what he must have gone through when he was asked to exile, on a day, when the entire Ayodhya was busy preparing for his coronation. Imagine his plight when he could not attend his father's funeral, as he had to move from one jungle to another. A would-be king, the queen, and his devoted brother, living a hermit life, in the most challenging and dangerous environments, sounds exciting in storybooks. But, going through this every day, for fourteen years straight, putting up a brave smile is beyond human, by any standards.

And the worst was the kidnapping of Sita*ji*. The intense search carried out without any clue, or knowledge of the direction, requires an unthinkable level of courage and positivity. Defeating Ravana, the most powerful *Rakshshsa* (demon), by creating an army of monkeys and other amateurs, displays true leadership skills and valor in times of crisis.

For a moment, forget that he was 'God.' You will then see that this man was subjected to the most unfortunate events throughout his life, reasons enough for an ordinary human to conveniently dispose of his values and justify any wrongdoing. And that's what Ravana did. When he could not marry Sita, he abducted her. We, as individuals, have an equal probability of becoming both Ram or Ravana. The liability is on us!

Most individuals give up when pushed against the wall. They blame situations and people surrounding them. But only a few embrace adversities with a smile, exhibiting high standards of moralities and principles. And if, your heart desires such humility, if your mind yearns for such dignity, and if you ever want to use the traits he shows, in real-life situations, then yes, he truly is to be worshiped and considered God. Otherwise, going to a temple and bowing down to his statue is just another routine in a long list of daily chores. True prayer is your conduct outside the temple."

Raghav was lost in the conversation. All of his questions had vanished. All he could do was marvel at the profound knowledge of the man. He was not sure whether all his questions were answered. But he could realize, all his questions were slowly vanishing in thin air.

"Is it only the *Ram-Leela* where you are Hanuman?" he asked, dumbfounded. "You are so knowledgeable. You could be a philosophy professor or a leadership mentor! Could you please share your contact details with me?"

Hanuman smiled mischievously. He was about to say something, but the train's Public Address system announced that the next station was Kandivali, Hanuman's destination.

"Hey Ram, didn't realize the destination had arrived," Hanuman said as he got off his seat. "I pray, your destination arrives soon, too. May you believe in Ram, the one residing in you. My part is done. Got to go now."

Raghav was left astounded. It was all so mysterious, yet so meaningful.

Chapter 9

Sleep had eluded Raghav for the past two months, but this morning was different. His mother sat by his side for a good half hour before waking him, feeling content with the calmness radiating off his face.

"What's the time, *Maa*?" a sleepy Raghav asked his mother.

"It's ten o'clock."

Raghav stood up in a flash, "I didn't realize it was so late."

"And I haven't seen you sleep so well in a while now," said his mother smiling, "freshen yourself up. I will make some tea, and then I have a small work to get done."

"What is it, *Maa*?" Raghav asked

"The tube light in the kitchen is not working. I guess it needs to be replaced. Need to look for an electrician," mother said as she went to the kitchen to make Raghav's favorite cardamom tea.

"I don't know any electrician, will look for one. The neighbors might know someone, or else I will have to go to a hardware store." he thought to himself, continuing, "I don't understand this. Here, there are many people like me, looking for technicians and there they are desperate for work. There should be a link. Someone or something to bridge this gap. Something like a platform of sorts."

Raghav dove deep into thought, as he stared at a jigsaw piece, trying to figure out where it fits. Vague ideas, ran haphazardly through his mind. Soon, his thoughts had gained momentum, as they got ready to soar. He immediately picked up his phone and called Lucky, "Hey, need to see you urgently!" he said.

Lucky, still on a sixty-day countdown, got anxious,

"Is everything okay?" he asked.

"Yes, I guess, I will let you know when we meet."

After Jhanvi shifted to Chennai, their meeting place too shifted to a small cafe in Juhu, near Lucky's residence. Unlike Cafe Mysore, this place was a contemporary, clutter-free, and happening place. A favorite among youngsters, this place served a variety of delicacies, some also a fusion of Italian and Mexican food, with fancy names.

Lucky, restless as ever, sipped his favorite hot-chocolate, as he tried calming himself down. He sat on a chair near the counter. The memory of Raghav's carelessness, of the previous day, kept playing in his mind repeatedly. It was for the first time in years that he had lost his cool with anyone. And Raghav too had no option, but to hear Lucky out, which he was prepared for, even today.

Raghav arrived in time and sat on a chair opposite Lucky.

"I am calling Jhanvi. I had asked her to keep herself free," he has said, as he connected to Jhanvi. She answered the call, and they could see her sitting in the office cafeteria.

"I have something positive that I want to share," Raghav was done feeling sorry for himself and got straight to the point.

Jhanvi, in her excitement, asked, "What's the news? I am dying to hear it!"

Lucky, although a little surprised, asked, "Did you get an offer from somewhere?"

"No offer, and from now on, I'll only say 'no' to any offer," Raghav replied.

He had never looked so confident. Not even during a presentation at work.

Jhanvi could notice this confidence in his body language.

Lucky, on the other hand, stretched his hand across the table, touched Raghav's forehead, "Are you okay?" he asked jokingly, continuing, "You must be having a fever. Did you get enough sleep last night?"

"I don't have time for this crap. Let me get straight to the point." Raghav said seriously.

"Tell me, which resource does India have in abundance?" he asked.

Lucky and Jhanvi, stared at each other, competing for the most puzzled look.

Raghav continued, "People call it population. I call it human resources; skilled, semi-skilled, unskilled, and all other types. The lifelong worry for them and the economy at large is common. They do not get enough employment opportunities, sometimes even for months. This impacts the GDP directly. And ironically, there still are many people who are looking for jobs, but have a difficult time finding any. So, at one end, there is a huge amount of unattended work, and at the other end, there is a huge amount of undiscovered potential, and whoever bridges this gap will not only do good business, but will also contribute to the cause." Raghav said as he saw the amazement on Lucky and Jhanvi's faces.

"I am looking to create a common platform, or to be precise, a website, and a mobile app. All a person will have to do then, is fill in their details, with their area of expertise. So whenever there is a requirement for any work, the end-user just needs to access the whole list of resource persons, area-wise, and skill-wise. This will connect them to each other, and the job will get done!"

Lucky jumped off his chair, shouting, "Eureka!"

The cozy couple, seated on the table next to them, were embarrassed, like how they would be, if they were seen by their parents. They instantly got off the table and moved to the one in the corner, looking awkwardly at Lucky.

Yet, for Lucky, they didn't exist.

"It's such a great idea!" Lucky exclaimed happily.

Before he could say anything further, Jhanvi interrupted him.

"It's a good idea, but to execute it into a business, we need to work out a comprehensive plan," she said, playing the devil's advocate, "Statistics say, nearly 70% of Indian start-ups fail within one year of being tagged as 'The future of Business,'"

Raghav, who was all charged up, was not willing to budge.

"You know why these start-ups fail?" Raghav asked

"Because, they just blindly replicate their business model through international models, serving half-baked edition for the Indian market, without considering aspects such as, local constraints, contexts, and requirements," he added, continuing, "A business needs to think differently, innovatively. Every country, era, and even area, has its unique challenges that require unique solutions. These challenges should be considered opportunities, that can be converted into unique business ideas. And if one can do this with utmost honesty, then I don't see any fear of failure!" he exclaimed confidently.

Jhanvi was trying to stay pragmatic as opposed to Raghav's optimism. She was happy, but worried too.

"Do you have any idea of how much capital would be required? How would you arrange it? Any visible horizon for break-even?" Jhanvi asked skeptically.

Raghav didn't have an answer to this.

"Right now, I only know that I don't know everything. And identifying your ignorance is the first step towards intelligence. I want to keep it simple! I will make a small team, and do the groundwork. Then, I'll complete the coding and come up with a prototype application for perhaps only one Mumbai suburb." Raghav replied, adding, "If everything goes as planned, then we will approach someone for funds. The timeline for all this is three months, maximum. There's no math to it. Just that I can survive only for the next three months on the final settlements I received, and if needed, we will use my savings."

Raghav was determined, and was ready to face any challenge.

"I am ready to fund the initial requirements," Lucky spoke out in support.

"Money is required, and is a must. But, it can also rust a relationship, without even realizing it!" Raghav exclaimed. "Money is expensive, but friendship is priceless," he added.

"Oye, emotional *fatichar*," Lucky started laughing just as soon as he heard this. "I may be dumb and impulsive, but not as much as you think. Let me remind you that I am the fourth generation to inherit my family's business. So, I am not lending money to my friend Raghav, but investing in an idea which looks like a good business opportunity. Now, I understand why I was so reluctant to join the family business." Lucky reflected.

"Things were ready for me on a silver platter. All support systems, conducive enough, to help me succeed, but there was one thing I was missing. The freedom to fail!

The game is worth winning, only when there is a chance of failing. I aspired to learn it my way, fail my way, and, if at all, there was any success along the way, to own it proudly one day," his voice throbbed with excitement.

"It's my day!" he exclaimed proudly.

All this while, Jhanvi remained quiet. Her eyes were moist as she held back her tears.

"I wish I was lucky enough to get some shares," she said as she choked.

Raghav gently rolled his fingers over the screen.

"You can own our company's shares, Jhanvi!" Lucky chipped in time.

Jhanvi looked surprised.

"I am serious, guys!" Raghav exclaimed, continuing, "Let me explain! As we start on, I reckon, we'll have to fight on multiple fronts, explore unknown territories, and at the same time, work for unique solutions. In this ordeal, there is a high chance that we may forget about the prerequisite, the product itself!"

He paused, proudly announcing, "So, here comes in Ms. Jhanvi! You will be the CEO of our company, with thirty-three percent shareholdings. Anyway, you're already bored in Chennai, so let's put your spare time to a noble cause, post office hours."

Jhanvi was pleasantly surprised by the proposal, but not without a couple of doubts.

"Let's be realistic. Turning this around in three months looks impossible. Besides, you need a technical team to work out the modules, do the coding, carry out quality checks, fix bugs, and the final prototype, and so on! Where will we get the manpower from? And even if we get it, we'll need PCs, hardware, and of course the office space. The higher you go up, will the horizon get wider?" Jhanvi asked worriedly.

None of them had all the answers, but all of them were equally determined to face any questions. Friendship is like a life seen through a kaleidoscope. The glass pieces within, are all broken, scattered, and lonely. But the lens of friendship creates the most wonderful designs out of them.

"Tell me one thing, Raghav" Lucky got inquisitive, "How did everything change for you in a single night?" he asked

"Can we know the reason for this miracle?"

"It's actually a little strange," Raghav started as Lucky, and Jhanvi were both ears.

"Yesterday, I met Hanumanji. I mean a guy playing the role of Hanumanji in *Ram-Leela*' while on my way home." he added.

"Do you know what the 'Geeta' is?"

"Yes, it's a spiritual discourse between Krishna and Arjuna," Lucky answered simply.

"That's true. But there is more to it than just that." Raghav said, and added, "Let me elaborate. Any intellectual, participative debate, dissolving all your questions, evolving eternal truth, is termed as 'Geeta' as per the '*Shashtra*.' The 'Bhagavad Geeta' is the pinnacle of such enlightening discussions. There are many more captivating debates like this, such as, the Ashtavakra Geeta between Sage Ashtavakra and King Janak, which is equally illuminating."

"Hmmm,"

"I don't like to exaggerate," Raghav was finding it difficult to express himself.

"But yesterday, I had my 'Geeta moment,' he added.

Jhanvi and Lucky both looked bewildered.

"I argued a lot with him over my crisis, the pain, and the sufferings every human being goes through in general. Mainly, the questions bothering me from the last sixty days, and they all flared up. And without even realizing, he started dissolving all my queries, one after the other. The awakening came in the wake of knowing Lord Ram, his sufferings, and his misfortune just like any other person on Earth. Understanding Ramayana from a human standpoint was a real eye-opener. It gave me a new meaning of divinity, a new meaning of my own life. The way he managed to sail through all the adversities with all his humility and humanity, is not only commendable but also implementable. My perspective of life has changed forever. Instead of making hue and cry, now I want to say 'Let's try!'"

There was silence. Both, exclamation and question marks flashed on the faces of the other two.

Jhanvi broke the silence, saying, "The story is fascinating. Although, I don't really think that person is an ordinary man working in a *Ram-Leela*! I am not sure, how you would have come out of this crisis, had you not met him. Whatever maybe the case; to me, he surely is God's messenger."

Lucky, broke his silence after quite a while, saying, "Do you think this is some kind of a mystery? A miracle, maybe?"

Raghav plainly nodded his head, while Lucky tried to rationalize this situation.

"We are all logical people. Even the software we develop doesn't work without logic, then where is the question of acceptance by the mind. What are you thinking, Raghav?" Lucky asked.

Raghav summarised, "Our eyes can't see atoms. It doesn't mean they don't exist. We can't reach for the stars in a far off galaxy. It doesn't mean they are not there. The limit of existence is zero to infinity, much beyond our imagination. We just need to zero our ego, and the infinite existence is ready to embrace us.

Hopefully, we'll meet him again someday. As of now, let's brace ourselves for the challenge at hand. The next few months are going to be the most exciting and decisive period for us."

Raghav's phone rang, interrupting the conversation. Presuming it to be yet another telecall, he put it on the speakerphone.

"Hi, Raghav. How are you? This is Shefali from Accord Inc."

"I am fine," Raghav said, squeezing his eyes.

"I called to say that you are selected for the job!"

"Oh, is it?" Raghav was surprised. Lucky got off his chair, while Jhanvi was stunned.

"But, as far as I remember, Mr. Kuldeep rejected me yesterday for not sharing the Syntel data."

"Yes, I know that. He was just testing you. That's his style! The only criterion for him is integrity. I think you won him over with that. He wants you to join immediately!"

Raghav looked at Lucky and Jhanvi, but the dilemma in their minds wrinkled their foreheads.

He had finally arrived at the destination he was searching for the past two months. However, for him, it was a crossroads. At one side was the safe and secure path, which was ready to welcome him with open arms. While on the other side, was the road less traveled, an unknown territory, full of uncertainty.

Destiny is a comedian! It changes the lock, the moment you've found the key to the old one.

It's crucial to make decisions, though. Decisions may bring failure, but procrastination guarantees failure.

This decision was critical. Logic works on the past for a conclusion. For future, you must follow your intuition. He gazed outside the coffee shop as he saw a blind man crossing the road with a stick in his hand. Raghav had made his decision.

"I am really sorry, ma'am, but I am on a different journey now," he said.

The blind man safely crossed the road instinctively.

Chapter 10

The enterprise bug had bitten, and beaten them well. The symptoms were infectious. The very next day, Raghav was ready with his step-by-step execution plan, which he explained to his partners over a conference call.

"1. Carry out a survey and prepare a comprehensive list of skilled, semi-skilled persons working in Borivali. The primary source of information - hardware store, and personal contacts. Also, look for people working in under-construction projects and maintenance projects. Responsibility – myself.

2. Start creating awareness about the application and its benefits. Responsibility – myself.

3. Look out for a rental space for the office, capable of accommodating at least 6-7 technical staff members. We need to recruit technical staff that can start immediately. Arrange for office, set up laptops, printers, and networking, including furniture, etc. Responsibility – Lucky.

This is going to be the biggest challenge, as we need to spend every rupee cautiously.

4. Prepare the activity flow; divide it into modules, and initiate with coding requirements. Jhanvi needs to keep it ready by the time we get the technical staff. Responsibility – Jhanvi."

"This task looks so simple," Lucky said, smiling, "The only problem is that we have to do it ourselves. You need at least someone to blame the goof ups on, man!" he added.

The air was filled with excitement, but nervousness too. The responsibility factor was slowly sinking into their systems. There was no one to blame, and no one to guide. Their first step on the road less traveled. One mistake from your end, and everything is gone. The difference between an entrepreneur and an employee is the appetite for risk. People with the highest intellect and qualification are found to be working for the 'not-so-qualified' ones for the same reason.

"And last but not least, the timeline for this is 15 days," Raghav said, as he concluded the meeting.

Raghav shut down his laptop, stepped out of his room, and headed straight to the hardware store. The store was a little more crowded than usual today. Raghav waited patiently for his turn, carefully observing all the customers at the counter. With stains of colors splashed all over a man's clothes, one could easily make out that he was a painter, undertaking house painting works. His order arrived, and the helper packed the tins of paint, turpentine, and scrubbing papers, among other things, in a gunny bag. The cashier was faster than a microprocessor, while calculating the amount. The computerized invoice followed much later. Another man was still in the queue after this, carrying a huge bag pack on his shoulders. At first glance, he looked like a food delivery guy, but he wasn't. The items that came out of his bag, made Raghav wonder.

Every crisis comes with its advantages too. The fact that it fuels up your survival instincts, propelling you to live life to the fullest, is really fascinating.

Raghav's mind worked sharp, like an antenna catching ideas at every possible place, and situation. Some strange thoughts soon started tickling his mind, as well.

The person in front of Raghav, was a salesman from a pipe company explaining some unique features of their newly launched products. The demonstration was completed within a few minutes. He then packed his bag and headed towards his motorbike, parked under a tree.

"Yes, sir, what do you want?" the person at the counter asked Raghav.

"Umm, I'll be back," Raghav said as he turned and rushed to the sales guy.

"Hey!" Raghav shouted.

The guy, a bit confused, turned his head slightly to check if someone called him from behind.

"I am talking to you, my friend, please wait," Raghav said as he went closer.

"I believe, you are working as a sales representative for a pipe company?"

"Yes, but who are you?"

"May I know your name, please?"

"Mangesh"

"Do you work on a fixed salary or incentives?"

"On incentive, but, who are you, man? Why are you asking me these things?"

"Oh, I am sorry!" Raghav realized that he hadn't introduced himself. He added, "I run a business, but can't go into details now. However, long story short, I've got a good proposal for you."

The suspense increased.

"Mangesh, how would you like to earn five to seven hundred rupees more every day? That too, without having to strain yourself too much."

Mangesh was intrigued.

"Tell me more," he told Raghav

"Look, my company is preparing a database of all technicians like electricians, plumbers, painters, carpenters, and the likes, who work as freelancers. Since you must be visiting many hardware stores a day, it's easy for you to collect details of technicians working in that vicinity. We'll also require some additional details. I will devise a mechanism soon. If you are willing to work more, I am willing to pay you five rupees per contact. Collecting a hundred contacts a day should not be a challenge for you. This means 500 rupees a day, and fifteen thousand a month."

Raghav was always good at making a presentation. He could see how Mangesh's eyes sparkled. Bread is good, but with butter on top, it always tastes better.

"I am up for it, but only with a single condition," Mangesh responded, adding, "The payment needs to be done on a daily basis."

"That's reasonable," Raghav said as he settled the deal. "We'll start the work from tomorrow. I need to iron out the details we need, and most importantly, how to get them."

Their cell numbers were exchanged as both shook hands.

Chapter 11

Raghav and Lucky were logged in, waiting for Jhanvi to join. The conference call meeting was fixed for every day at 8 PM.

"Hey, would anyone like to have a coffee?" Jhanvi said as she smiled at Raghav, pointing to the coffee mug in her hand. She relaxed on the sofa. Raghav smiled back. He had gifted her the coffee mug, when she was promoted.

Their love was pocket friendly. Simple things like a coffee mug, chocolates, or a pen were good enough to be considered a gift. A long walk along the Marine Drive promenade, eating *Bhel-Puri* at Chowpaty followed by ice cream, was all it took for them to call it a romantic date.

"So, what's the update?" Raghav asked like a school kid, who, having finished his assignment, was ready to make fun of the non-performers.

Lucky started with his updates, "I've inquired with some of the estate agents in my vicinity. But, the response is not encouraging. None have a place for an office. Besides, due to us being unsure of continuing the lease beyond three months, it is completely detrimental. People prefer a longer period. A minimum of eleven months." he said with dejection, continuing, "I am visiting each of them tomorrow, so will keep you posted, but, it looks like, we are facing roadblocks even before the beginning of the road."

"Use the roadblocks as stepping stones! We have no option, Lucky," Raghav tried encouraging Lucky. "Let's talk something positive. I've identified a person for collecting the technicians' details across the suburb, and he said that we'd be ready with at least three thousand contacts in less than a month! And that too, at just fifteen thousand rupees."

"Wow! That's interesting," Jhanvi was all in praises.

"How did you do that?" Lucky was excited to know.

"Going by the conventional route, we would have required to hire a minimum of two recruits, train them and establish a supply chain for data collection. This would have taken us not less than a month," Raghav explained, continuing, "While I was at the hardware store, I noticed a salesman, who was familiar with the entire chain of hardware stores in the suburb. Also, he goes there regularly, and has a rapport with each of them. That's when I got an idea of leveraging it to our advantage. I approached him and cracked up a deal for five rupees per contact. He had no qualms in accepting the offer, as it gives him an additional income. So guys, fasten up. We are ready to take off!"

"Wow, that's great news, man!" Lucky said as he started singing, thumping his fist in the air. "*Hum Honge Kamyaaab...Hum Honge Kamyaab...*We will win!"

"How do you plan to collect the data? It needs to be structured," Jhanvi got back to business.

"I thought of the same, and we will work something out. Standard online forms are handy. But they are too generic, besides privacy is an issue. I need something exclusive to our system" Raghav started brainstorming ideas.

"I can code in a simple form, whose link can be circulated, and the details subsequently filled," Jhanvi came up with her solution. "The database will be exclusive and easy to sync with our program at a later date."

"Sounds good," Lucky replied.

Raghav liked the idea. "That's perfect, let's do it! But get it done by tomorrow morning, so I can give it to Mangesh, the salesman," he added.

"On it! Goodbye, guys." Jhanvi said as she left the meeting.

Chapter 12

Dreams do come true for all those who work while they dream!

Jhanvi stayed up the entire night. Even though the length of the coding was short, she kept a holistic approach, taking the future programming requirements into consideration. Setting the right tone is as important in a computer program as it is in a musical program.

For Lucky, although, being an insomniac, waking up early was a nightmare. During office days, half of his privilege leaves were used up against him in coming late.

But time changes, and it changes a lot in you. Today, Lucky was on the breakfast table, before others, greeted by a few surprised looks, with his mother inquiring about his well-being.

The nearest commercial hub to his place, was the Andheri link road, which had transformed tremendously over a decade. From a modest industrial area with bad roads, it now was home to numerous A-list corporates and media houses. The swanky showrooms of luxurious cars, lined up one after the other, adding their opulence to the surroundings.

Lucky glanced at his smart-watch. It was 10.30 AM now. He had reached before the agent.

The restlessness of the city had picked up the pace on the link road. The agent's office was in a lane, on the ground floor of an industrial estate. It was a small, yet functional space designed with good architectural sense.

The mirror covering the entire wall added more space visually. Mr. Tulsiani arrived at 11, in his white SUV. A middle-aged man, with shiny grey hair, he looked charming in his golden spectacles and all-white clothes. He removed his footwear at the entrance, and bowed to the Ganesha idol behind the reception counter.

He looked at Lucky and signaled him to follow him inside the cabin. Mr. Tulsiani occupied his chair behind the huge white table, while Lucky sat on the visitor's chair.

The cabin had an all-white decor with a stone mural behind Mr. Tulsiani's chair, as he was fond of the color white.

"I am Lucky. I had called you yesterday," Lucky said nervously.

"You need a commercial space of 300 sqft, right?"

"Yes, sir."

"What company do you work for? I mean, do they need it for manufacturing or for something like a showroom?"

"I don't work for any company. I own a company," Lucky said, hesitantly.

From Mr. Tulsiani's experience, he could easily gauge Lucky's novice approach.

"Ours is a small IT startup. As a result, we need space for at least 5 or 6 programmers, for around three to four months. And needless to say, ours is a very tight budget," Lucky said, understanding the meaning of the word 'inferiority complex,' probably for the first time.

"Firstly, the average rent out here is around fifty thousand a month. Secondly, no one would be interested in leasing for less than eleven months. And even if we find one, you'll have to shell out at least five lakhs for the deposit, brokerage, statutory charges, and interior works. I am sure you must have done your research," Mr. Tulsiani spoke empathetically.

"Yes, you are right. I need to do some more research," Lucky said, as he shook hands and left his office.

The task was tougher than he had thought. He also met a couple of other agents in the vicinity, but the result was a no brainer.

All these years, he never had to bother about any price tags. Be it his toy car as a kid, or getting a sports car as a graduation present, he had it all. But, the abundance of oxygen is ignored with every breath. The acknowledgment comes only when it is pumped through a ventilator. Lucky got emotional, and felt really grateful for his parents.

His train of thought was interrupted by Raghav's phone call.

"What's up, Lucky? I am done with my part. I have given the link of the online form to Mangesh, and we will have to wait till evening for the initial data."

"Things are not positive here," Raghav gauged Lucky's frustration, as Lucky continued, "The rent everywhere, is beyond our budget. I met with different agents, but the results remained unchanged. Some people even laughed at our budget. I'm not sure, how to get through."

"I can understand! It must have seemed like you're ordering a *vada-pav* in a five-star restaurant. Haha!" Raghav started laughing, trying to ease out the tension. "We have to reorient ourselves. Raghav said. Try somewhere near my place. We only need a functional space for an office, not for a showroom. The location doesn't matter."

Lucky was in sync, "You are right. The location doesn't matter. I will come over there tomorrow and start searching."

The evening meetings went on as per schedule, every day. The data from Mangesh has started coming in. To validate, Raghav started calling some of them randomly, understanding their way of working, and taking their feedback on the online platform. Some were positive, some doubtful. Nevertheless, things were gaining momentum.

Jhanvi had prepared the entire program flow, the front end interface, along with the back-end requirements, each broken into different modules. Ten days of painstaking detail, and fierce brainstorming, is what it took to arrive at this concurrence.

Every day brought forth a new lesson in entrepreneurship. It's easy to manage your constraints, but managing constraints beyond your control are not everyone's cup of tea. A true entrepreneur is the one who converts these constraints into opportunities, to grow beyond boundaries.

The search for the right property around Raghav's place had started. The hunt grew stronger each day, as nothing matched the required criteria. None of the fifteen agents they approached could give them any breakthrough. They could not blame anyone but themselves. The days slipping out of hands, gave them sleepless nights.

Visiting agents in the morning, and commercial places in the afternoon, while taking a quick bite at *Rushimukh* restaurant, in between, had become their daily routine.

It was a hot afternoon, and the frustration was creeping in. Lucky asked the waiter to turn the tower fan towards them.

"The fifteen-day target of finding an office place is about to hit the deadline. Neither is there a place, and nor do we have any idea how we'll arrange the IT set up, let alone hiring programmers!"

Raghav had no answer.

"We only have two options. Either we call it quits, or I approach my dad for more funding."

"Life has got us here, so life only will get us through," Raghav said, trying to remain optimistic.

"But, we need results, and we need them fast," Lucky grew restless.

"I think, I can be of some help to you," they heard a voice from behind.

Both of them stood puzzled. The face behind the voice was still not visible.

"Sorry, who are you?" Lucky questioned, getting off his seat.

"Can I join you?" the voice asked, as a hand waved at them from the table behind. The huge column between the tables still blocked their view.

The person got up from his table and stood in front of them. A young man, in his thirties, dressed simply, with neatly combed hair and a *tilak* on his forehead. He looked modest, yet confident.

"I am going to punch you if you are up to some prank!" Lucky was annoyed.

Raghav waved his hand at Lucky, signaling him to calm down.

The man pulled up a chair, and sat in the aisle.

"Care to introduce yourself?" Lucky asked, annoyed.

"As far as I can tell, both of you are from the IT sector, and currently trying to set up your own startup, right?"

They were checkmated by a pawn in the first move. They realized how foolish it was to judge anything by the cover.

The surprise, although, was far from over yet.

"So, I understand you are looking for an office space. And an IT setup, programmers and office interiors are the next critical priorities, right?" the man said as he smiled proudly.

They had no option, but to agree with him.

"But, you didn't answer my question. Who are you? And how do you know all this?" Lucky asked inquisitively

"My name is MS. The name is long. Thus people prefer to call me by my initials. I work as a manager in Classic Computer Classes, just above this restaurant. This is my regular lunch outlet, and I have been overhearing your conversations the past few days," he paused, allowing them to react.

"I can help you with all your requirements," he added.

With their eyes wide open, both got to the edge of their seats.

"The cost of renting a new commercial place, along with the costs of the IT infrastructure and interiors, would cost no less than three lakhs. Hiring a single programmer will cost you at least twenty-five thousand a month. With overheads, the cost will run up to another three lakhs a month, correct?"

Both simply nodded their head in dismay.

"Here is my solution", he paused to look at them, as they looked at each other.

"The students at our computer classes range from kids to housewives to engineering students. While others are manageable, the engineering students are caught in a soup. The professor guiding them on their project work, met with an accident recently, and is out of action for at least two months, leaving them in limbo. The experience of a project work matters more to them than their academics, as it gives them an upper hand during campus interviews lined up in a couple of months from now."

The story slowly started unfolding in their minds.

"So here's my offer. I will offer you a full-fledged office, with a ready IT setup, and of course, programmers. All you have to do, is teach them your programming needs as their project work," MS had laid his offer on the table.

"And, needless to say, the entire package is free for you! Only, the constraint is, the students come in the evening, post their college hours," he added.

"You are absolutely spot on, my friend. We have no issues with the timing." Raghav said, grabbing his hand in joy.

I have one question I'd like to ask, though, if you don't mind," Lucky asked, as he looked to clear a final query.

"How are you benefitting amid all this? Are there any hidden expenses?! I mean, let's be practical. What favor do you need in return?"

MS burst into laughter just as soon as he heard this. "It's a win-win for all. The owner gets rid of a business hurdle. You get your startup ready. The students get the knowledge they need. And I get the satisfaction of helping someone. Do you think money can ever buy that satisfaction?"

Both jumped off their seats, giving each other, a high-five. Another hand stretched out to join them. It was MS's.

"Let's party!" Lucky shouted ecstatically.

"The party will follow. Let's celebrate with ice cream first," Raghav said, waving at the waiter.

"I'll have chocolate choco chips. Double scoop," Lucky ordered in excitement.

"Badam-Pista for me," Raghav ordered, now looking at MS, he asked, "And what will you have?"

"My favorite is Kesar-Pista, and it is Saturday today," MS said, smiling mischievously.

"You can start working from Monday evening," he added.

Chapter 13

The mood was ecstatic. After a long time, Raghav, Lucky, and Jhanvi were discussing regular things, and not a business.

"I still can't believe this," Jhanvi's face glowed.

"Yes, it still hasn't sunk in for me either," Raghav reciprocated, adding, "Thanks to our man, MS."

"I could never imagine someone coming out of the blue and helping us sail through. I misjudged him at first, and I am glad I was proven wrong!" Lucky confessed, adding, "Running short of words to praise him, man!"

"Guys, let's relax for now, and prepare ourselves for the next two months. They are going to be crucial for us," he said, turning to Jhanvi.

"You will play the most crucial role from here on, Jhanvi! The quality of the product we offer will decide the quality of our company's future. It has to be simple and user friendly, with an organized back-end, that retrieves data in a flash. The earlier we make it, the better it is. On Monday, when Lucky and I reach Classic Computers, we will assess the IT set up and arrange video conferencing. The orientation will start by seven. Will you be ready with your presentation by then, Jhanvi?"

"Yes. I'll try to be back home by six."

Raghav and Lucky reached the place, the next day. Raghav looked at the board, and kept repeating it to himself.

"The Classic Computer Classes!" Raghav thought, climbing the narrow staircase, "The owner must be fond of poetry to come up with such an alliterated name!"

Upon reaching upstairs, they saw two residential flats combined to set up the classes. The open shoe rack placed in the narrow corridor, was loaded with a variety of footwear. The logo was etched on the semi-transparent glass door at the entrance. Upon opening the door, they saw the reception. It was a cramped space, with only a small reception table and two chairs.

"Welcome, Raghav and Lucky," a voice greeted them from the ceiling speakers.

A bit amazed, they could identify, it was MS's voice.

"Please walk inside the door to your left," He instructed them to follow.

Raghav located a door handle on an otherwise seamless laminated partition. It opened into a small cabin with compact furniture, including an executive chair, a table, with two chairs in front. The cabin, though, was empty. The mystery was building up.

"Hello? Is anybody there?" Lucky whispered.

"I am with you always!" MS's voice came from somewhere behind the table.

Both Raghav and Lucky saw a figure slowly emerging from the other side of the office table. He was MS, smiling at them. Wiping his hands with a tissue, he offered them to sit.

"How did you know, it was us at the reception?" Lucky couldn't stop himself from asking.

"Oh, yes, I didn't mention it, but I've got a *Tri-Netra,* a third eye. With this, I can see everything," MS added to the suspense.

They both looked at each with more perplexity.

"Hey, friends, don't take me so seriously. I was kidding," MS said, as he started laughing. He turned the monitor on the table, "This is my third eye. All my CCTV cameras are connected to this!"

"And yes, I was just checking the Public Address system by calling you when I instructed you. It's working well in the reception. However, it seems to have some problems in the classroom. I was just fixing the cable below."

The mystery turned into a logical reality.

"Come, let me show you the classrooms," MS said, as he got up from his chair and began taking them around.

A few bedrooms were converted into classrooms. One living room was converted into a computer lab, with about ten linear workstations along the periphery. Every square inch was utilized to the fullest.

"That's such a great setup!" a relieved Raghav said, "Lucky, can check the configuration of each system? I hope you don't mind, MS*Ji*."

"I would certainly mind, if you spoil my name by adding '*Ji*.'" MS smiled at him, "You may verify everything, and here is the list of systems, with their configurations," he said, handing over a printout.

Lucky's admiration was turning into respect for MS.

"Do we have a set up for video conferencing? Our third associate, Jhanvi, is operating from Chennai for now," Raghav enquired.

"Don't worry at all. I am here to connect everyone, my friend!" MS expressed heartily.

"We'll never forget your help, MS," Raghav said as he smiled. "No applying '*Ji*' anymore, okay."

The setting was complete. A large TV screen was connected to one of the computers, serving as a conference screen. Luckily, Jhanvi was able to finish her day early, and connected quickly, flashing a big smile on the screen. The students gathered in the computer lab. The clock showed 6.55 PM, and it was the time to begin.

MS briefly introduced Raghav and Lucky.

"Hi, friends!" Raghav took the lead, continuing, "It's really exciting to be here. It reminds us of our college days! We are truly missing those anxieties of assignments, submissions, practicals, vivas, and of course, the results.

Life is funny. Life is stupid! Today's nightmares make beautiful memories tomorrow. So live in this moment, give it your best."

The mood in the room got lighter, as smiles began turning brighter.

"Meet my colleague, Lucky," he put his arm around Lucky's shoulder. "Lucky and I will assist you in programming occasionally, while Ms. Jhanvi will be guiding you mostly," Stepping aside, pointing at the screen, "She is currently based in Chennai. Over to you, Jhanvi!"

Jhanvi waved at everyone from the screen, "Hi guys. I am not going to take too much of your time, and neither am I going to start confusing you with coding puzzles. What I am going to do is to take you through a simple, step by step presentation on the basics of coding. But before that, let's have a quick round of introduction. Like it or not, we all have to bang our heads with each other for the next couple of months. So I guess it's always better to get acquainted with those heads!" she added.

There were six girls and four boys. All of them introduced them one by one. Girls were Foram, Ria, Hasti, Prajakta, Mia, Urmi, Zaira, and Soham, Raj, Zeeshan, and Dev were the boys.

Jhanvi quickly wrapped up her slides on the program cycle, starting from establishing requirements, product designs, coding, testing, and bug fixing, live run, and maintenance. What followed, was more important.

She started an informal session with some lighter questions about their college life and group dynamics, things like who is always late for the class? Who is the ATKT king/queen? Who is the sportsperson?

The otherwise dull and drooping faces suddenly came alive, pulling each other's legs, and cracking jokes. Talent is always the second-best ingredient of the success of any project. The first one is always the teamwork, and the synergy amongst them. Jhanvi had implemented this on the very first day.

The flight was ready to take-off.

Raghav and Lucky were relaxed about the coding. They now had to focus on two other crucial challenges. First on the list, were the marketing requirements; to create a buzz and excitement for the app, and among potential users, about the launch. Raghav looked after this, as Lucky assumed another important task.

The app, once ready, would still only cater to a small, localized area, reaching out to only a few technicians and skillsets. However, it would be successful, and meaningful, only if it reached out to every corner of the country, creating millions of job opportunities. While the initial success would give the required thrust, a lot of fuel will still have to be pumped, in order to put the satellite into its desired orbit. Lucky, now, had to search for potential investors and venture capitalists to propel their mission to the next level. Thus, Raghav was the Chief Marketing Officer and Lucky, the chief Financial Officer.

For any enterprise to be successful, it is important to create a line of responsibilities, delegate them to a matching profile, and, most importantly, entrust them with full authority.

With a list of technicians registered through the link, Raghav started calling them individually, getting their feedback, and understanding their actual requirements. The common denominator of all feedback was to provide a multilingual interface. Raghav immediately informed Jhanvi to make the necessary changes.

Nearly eighty to a hundred calls were made daily. Rather than advertising the app, Raghav was hearing, the ones he'd called. This not only built trust amongst the technicians and workers, but also gave Raghav a lot of insight in return. Half the customers' problems were solved, the moment you align yourself with their problems, rather than pitching your product.

Lucky, on the other hand, was busy preparing a list of investors, venture capitalists, PE funds who were actively involved in funding the startup. He had a lot of data crunching to do, while working out numbers, growth projection, break-even analysis, and ROI, under various scenarios, and be ready with a concise, corporate presentation.

Each day dawned with a new question, and each night slept with a unique answer. The uncertainties of life are not always to be solved; for they are to be lived for as well.

You may or may not find an answer to every situation, but life certainly looks back at you, meaningfully. The destination must be the goal, but the scenery along the way shouldn't be missed either. After all, on the way is where you spend most of your time. The destination is just another milestone in the journey, incidentally, the last one.

The destination was indeed, insightful.

"I want both of you to be in class tomorrow, at 7 PM, sharp!" Jhanvi exclaimed on the video call, as the students surrounded her. Raghav and Lucky could hardly hear her voice, as the happy noise of the students' overpowered everything.

"What's the news, Ma'am?" Lucky asked.

"See it, to believe it!" all said in unison.

To Raghav and Lucky, it seemed like, they'd entered a sports bar after the world cup win. As soon as they entered, they were welcomed by a loud cheer.

"It's finally done!" Jhanvi shouted from behind the screen. "We have finally completed the project. I'm dying to show you the live run."

Hip-Hip-Hurray, Hip-Hip-Hurray!" Lucky shouted like a little kid.

For once, Raghav flashed a big smile on his face. "Let's run through it first."

All was set. Half the students logged in as dummy technicians and workers, using different languages. The other half acted as the end-users, logging in for different requirements.

Jhanvi, here, was like an orchestra conductor playing the perfect symphony. The symphony ended on a perfect note, followed by applause.

"Three cheers for Jhanvi Ma'am."

"Thank you so much, Ma'am."

"All because of you, Ma'am."

The students reacted, expressing their gratitude. It was hard for Jhanvi to be able to control her emotions. The moist corner of her eyes, sparkled like a pearl in an oyster. It is a delightful sight to see tears rolling down smiling lips, the kind of pain personified in the poem!

Her wish to be present there, with the class, Lucky, and of course Raghav, was stronger than ever.

Raghav, seeing her in tears, embraced his arms around the air, like hugging her.

"I congratulate all of you, and thank you for taking the first step forward towards a giant leap. Jhanvi truly deserves all the praises and applauses. But, let me tell you, there is one person more praiseworthy than her, without whom our dreams would have never seen the light of the day," he paused, while announcing.

"And it's the class manager, MS! Let's call him and acknowledge his huge contribution."

"I think, he is not here today. Let's check," a student pointed out.

All went to the reception.

"Where is MS? Is he in the cabin, or is he coming late today?" Lucky asked, as his inquisitiveness grew.

"No. He won't be coming anymore," the receptionist replied.

Everyone stood stunned.

"What?" a shocked Raghav asked, losing words.

"What are you saying?" Raghav was still unable to process this.

"He had come in the morning. Unfortunately, there is bad news. His brother met with an accident. I was the one who booked the tickets, as he had to rush to his native place immediately." the receptionist answered

"His number is switched off. It's probably a network issue!" Raghav tried calling his number constantly.

"Oh, the number won't work." the receptionist interrupted, adding, "This number is printed in every advertisement. Hence he returned the SIM card, for me to attend to inquiries."

Lucky lifted the paper that lay on the reception table. Upon seeing what was written on it, his expressions changed dramatically. He showed it to Raghav.

It was a spare copy of MS's ticket.

The name written on it spelled 'MARUTINANDAN SHUKLA – MS.'

Raghav and Lucky looked at each other in disbelief.

Chapter 14

God knows why people are so fascinated with video games, although, both exhibit a striking resemblance. By the time you can celebrate the completion of one level, other challenging tasks are ready to welcome you in the next round.

The battle had now opened up on many fronts. While it was important to manage the momentum gained by registered technicians, generating enthusiasm amongst the users was essential. The biggest challenge for creativity was to work within the constraints of the budget. Every penny had to be spent judiciously, to be able to sustain through the uncertain gestation period. Distributing hand-outs, along with newspapers in the local area, proved to be an effective and economical solution. Social media was also being used to its fullest potential. Mass messages on social networking apps, blogging to creating awareness for the app, initiating debates on topics like, "Can Technology Work for Technicians?" among others, created a reasonable buzz across social media platforms.

Jhanvi was managing the post-implementation glitches, incorporating received feedbacks with the help of students. However, the students were also busy preparing for their exams and campus interviews.

Lucky was ready with his final presentation to be presented to a list of possible investors. But, two critical questions remained unanswered.

"Who makes the decisions in the organization?"

And

"How to reach out to that person?"

For most critical questions of life, there are no predefined answers. Neither can cognizance come to your rescue. Your attitude and preparedness to face any questions as it comes are what determine the outcome.

The target set to achieve this milestone was two months. There was no particular math behind this, except for the fact that their funds wouldn't last beyond this. The race against time was getting bigger by the day, and so were the hurdles!

"Guys, need your inputs on this," Lucky said, as he led the conference call.

"I've already shared the presentation with you. The list of probable investors is in place. But, what we are missing is a very vital link that can connect us to the right person.

Currently, I am trying to crawl through professional networking sites, trying to get some breakthrough. So far, I'm Lucky only by name!" Lucky said as he laughed at his own lame joke.

"Can we get in touch with anyone working in an organization who can show us the way," Raghav asked.

"Do you think, visiting their office and seeking an appointment can give us some mileage?" Jhanvi chipped in.

"I don't think so," Raghav replied unconvincingly.

"But, we have nothing to lose either. We might as well get some clue, who knows," he said, adding, "Let's take one step at a time. We start with Angel Finance and Pristine Capital. Both offices are in the same building. I'll see you tomorrow morning at 9.30."

It was a usually busy morning at Angels. The sun rays, piercing through the glass façade, ran across the marble-clad corridor, seemingly rushing to punch the "in time" before the employees. The air gushing out of the air conditioner vents were seemingly in a hurry to cool down every inch of the lobby as if it is also under pressure to achieve management target. The stream of water, in the granite water body, situated in the center, followed a controlled and predefined pattern.

Traditionally, nature has had a huge influence on man-made designs and ambiance. But, out here, the design completely dominated nature, confining it to fixed guidelines. The ambiance was not far behind either, looking as artificial as the people around, with fake smiles, protocol handshakes, and camouflaged characters. Do we still need more artificial intelligence?

Raghav was pleasantly surprised to see Lucky reach before him and wait in the reception lobby. The responsibility now overtook luck.

Raghav and Lucky, both sat there feeling awkward.

"Let me check it out, at the reception," Lucky said, as he headed straight to the reception. The reception table was probably as long as a cricket pitch, clad by veneer, and metal engraving on it.

"May I help you, sir?" One of the four receptionists sitting behind the desk asked Lucky.

"I want to meet Mr" Lucky tried his luck and made a wild guess, "Mr. Das, one who handles the startup funding at Angel."

"I am afraid there is no Mr. Das at Angel," The receptionist replied, scrolling through the database. "Are you sure about the name?" she asked

"In that case, who better than you to tell me who handles that division?" Lucky asked confidently.

"No idea, sir," the receptionist replied politely.

"Can you please check up at Pristine Capital?"

"No, sir, there isn't anyone by the name of Mr. Das there," she was now getting confused.

"I am sorry, Ma'am," Raghav interrupted. "To be honest, we have a small startup and wish to connect with someone that manages the portfolio either at Angels or Pristine. Can you please help us with this?"

"I am afraid, I can't, sir! We don't have these details. And even if we did, we couldn't have shared with a stranger. You know, how people take advantage of such information." she replied.

"I understand, but please help us if you know anything," Raghav replied, adding, "We shall be visiting the place regularly."

She nodded with a smile.

"Let's go to Apex Ventures, BKC. And if time permits, we have to cover CZ Global today, as well," Raghav told Lucky.

"The cab is five minutes away," Lucky replied, booking a cab.

"Let's move faster and try to reach before lunchtime, or else we will waste an hour."

Raghav rushed, as Lucky tried to keep up, accidentally missing the service ladder near the exit door. He almost barged into it, making it shake. By the time he recovered from this shock, a flying figure had landed in front of his eyes, coming face to face. He couldn't understand or believe what was happening. The person in front of him was smiling, holding a stick over his muscular shoulder. From his uniform, one could he was the housekeeping guy using the ladder.

"Oh, I am sorry. We didn't see you!" Raghav apologized to Lucky.

"Happens!" The person replied. Adding, "Sometimes the things we are looking for are too close to be noticed. They are near, and yet so far!

He then got poetic. "We set our eyes on the horizon, but miss the boat waiting at the shore, that takes us there. You need to slow down. Come back to the roots. Come back inside."

By the time, they could react, he was gone, climbing the ladder. They both looked at each other. A little surprised, and a bit confused!

Chapter 15

Lucky's cell rang, bringing them both back to reality. The cab driver was at the other end. It took them some time to cross the busy road. The cab was parked in a by-lane. The traffic along the route wasn't as bad, but not good enough to take them as quickly as they wished to be to the Apex Ventures office. They reached, but it was lunchtime. They had to wait for some time in the lobby.

They then informed their purpose of visit at the reception.

The receptionist was cordial enough to respond professionally, "I am not sure if the company is looking for any fresh investments. Nevertheless, you may please hand over your presentation to me. I'll forward it to the person concerned," she said.

"Thank you, ma'am," Lucky replied with a smile, adding, "Our details are mentioned in the presentation. However, we'll visit the place after a couple of days to bother you. We need your help."

Stepping out of the office, they felt relaxed. They weren't sure if their presentation would reach the right person, but at least someone had lent them a helping hand. And this was enough motivation for them at this time.

Sometimes, a small act of kindness, a simple positive response is what it takes to boost your morale. Everyone can't be influential enough to transform many lives. But it's always possible to spread positivity all around with small acts of kindness.

The response from CZ Global was not so encouraging. They had stopped making new investments, focusing completely on their current portfolio.

The dates on the calendar moved faster than usual. The hunt was eating up a significant amount of their time and energy.

The waiting lounge at Angels had become a part-time office for them. Raghav had become proficient in utilizing the waiting period in calling up technicians and analyzing their feedback. It was important to focus on customer responses that would generate more leads by word of mouth publicity. The only silver lining was that the numbers of customers were growing steadily every day.

Jhanvi was busy updating the app incorporating customer feedbacks, improving interface experience, and analyzing backup data. Things were getting better by day technically, although not practically.

It was almost a month since they'd started visiting these offices. The schedule was fixed. One day at Angel and Pristine, and the next at Apex. They'd now become familiar faces in the Angel and Pristine lobby. With each passing day, the frustration increased on their faces. Lucky was getting more restless by the day, biting nails and shaking legs. Suddenly, he grabbed Raghav's hand.

"Look, he is Mr. Rohit Mahajan, the CEO of Angels," he said, pointing to a profile picture on a website.

His career looked interesting. With a degree in architecture and post-graduation in management from IIM Ahmadabad, he had climbed the corporate ladder, faster than an elevator.

"I've seen him pass by a couple of times, mostly surrounded by his associates. We must intercept him right in the corridor and offer our proposal!" Lucky added.

"That's *hara-kiri*, suicide! Do you understand?" Raghav stood in disagreement.

"It's better to try and die, than wait and cry," Lucky did not budge.

"But remember, if we miss out by any chance, the doors will be closed forever!" Raghav warned Lucky.

"You talk as if there is someone on the other side of the door waiting to welcome us with open arms," Lucky said, unable to hide his frustration.

"But, I don't,"

Before Raghav could say anything, Lucky got up in a flash, and ran towards the exit.

A live demonstration of Murphy's Law was about to happen. He could see Mr. Rohit Mahajan heading towards the exit, talking to a couple of executives. All the executives, kept nodding their heads and faking smiles, looking their professional best. They suddenly stopped, seeing Lucky block their way, with his hands stretched out like a traffic cop. Baffled by this act, they didn't understand what was happening. Before they could react, Lucky started his mission.

"Rohit sir, I beg you to spare me a few minutes," he started with folded hands. "We have a small startup, and seek your valuable time to present briefly."

Mr. Rohit looked cool and unfazed. He was about to say something, when an executive grabbed Lucky by the shoulder, shouting, "Who the hell are you?"

"I know this is not appropriate, but please spare us some time. We have a great idea," Lucky pleaded.

"Do you have any idea who you are speaking to? Your idea must be as crude as your approach," The other executive lambasted Lucky, not wanting to lose an opportunity to impress his boss.

The security rushed in, while Raghav came running from the other side.

"Sir, I apologize on his behalf. We are a little frustrated as we were unable to get access to you" Raghav tried to calm them.

"And you thought our company achieves milestones by buying ideas from the streets?" the third executive chipped in, not wanting to be left behind in the quest to impress their boss.

Even a passer-by who tries his hands on a pick-pocket, ends up being beaten by the crowd. The present scene was its corporate version.

Mr. Rohit still kept his composure. He was about to intervene, but his phone rang, diverting his attention.

"Yes, Mr. Batra, we have already started. Should be there in half an hour," he replied politely.

"Let's move, guys. Mr. Batra doesn't like to wait!" he said, exiting the building. The car was waiting for him. The executives followed him in their cars.

Raghav and Lucky stood still at the gate, dejected. The cars kept moving further, and further away, fading from their sight, blurring their hope, and shredded it into pieces like a waste.

"I shouldn't have crossed the line," Lucky said, with guilt, adding, "I should have listened to you. You can't blame them. I am the problem, my impatience. I am so sorry, Raghav."

"Don't feel so bad, and upset," Raghav said, patting Lucky's back, and continued, "We failed, but at least we tried. Let's have faith. God helps those who help themselves."

"This is good for a moral science class in school. Ignorance was bliss! Maturity comes with its strong hands of logic, strangulating our innocence, and instinctive trust. Sometimes I really think whatever we studied is useless!"

"God has his plans to teach us things."

"Can I say something?" a voice approached them from behind.

Raghav turned his back and saw a muscular, young man, dressed in a blue and white uniform, standing behind them. He had some files in his hand.

Lucky was quick to recognize him. He was the same man who had fallen from the ladder, the other day. Judging by his face, he looked docile, yet very confident.

"Sorry, but we are not here looking for housekeepers for our home. We don't need your help." Lucky snapped sarcastically.

Raghav, although, didn't approve of his behavior and told him to keep quiet.

"Lucky, you are doing the same to him as that executive did to you. What is the difference? You can't judge someone by their appearance." Raghav said.

"I am really sorry," Lucky said, apologizing to the man. "I was frustrated. All roads are closing for us."

"That's the problem with us, my friend!" the man said, continuing, "When we pass through a scenic road, under the tree shades, we never think of being grateful, and thanking the ones who made it. Even when that road ends, we resort to blaming others for the road not being good enough. We take everything for granted! Instead of whining, doesn't it make more sense to try and make another road?"

Raghav never expected such profoundness from the man, who appeared so humble.

"Sir, my *mantra* is simple. Life is like traveling by a local train. Would you still cry if you missed a few overcrowded trains? Or will you prepare yourselves better to catch the next one?" the man asked.

"The train runs on a fixed schedule. You know when the next one will arrive. But life is not a local train journey," Lucky replied.

"But even rails have suffered major breakdowns, right?" the man was prompt in his response, and continued, "Do you know what happens during the breakdown?" he waited for them to react.

"What?"

"It is only after a breakdown, that one can repair the problem, may it be a fault or a wreckage," he replied, continuing, "This is vital for uninterrupted and prospective journeys, while the credit goes to the breakdowns. But we're so used to cursing the short term issues. Essentially, they are the ones that bring long term solutions." The man was cleverer than he looked.

Have you stopped using trains just because there was a breakdown for a few hours, among other troubles? When you can rely so much on a man-made system, then why can't you have more faith in God's system?"

Raghav and Lucky both were amazed to see the true spirit of a *Mumbaikar*. They could relate their situation to a local train journey and find the solution!

"I guess, you have some start-up and now want to get in touch with a few offices here," the man continued.

Both of them were equally surprised.

"You know a lot of things! A secret agent at work? Haha," Raghav exclaimed.

"Oh, no! I am just a common man, with some common sense," he said, raising the file in his hand, continuing, "I reckon this is your file. I found it yesterday below the sofa where you guys normally sit."

"That's so nice of you, buddy!" Raghav smiled.

"So, you read the file?" Lucky asked.

"Yeah, I was just trying to figure out whose file is it," the man replied.

"And you actually could figure out our exact status. Nice observation. You must be educated. Can you tell us something about yourself?" Raghav asked inquisitively.

"I am a graduate in agricultural sciences. Incidentally, I also nurture a dream like yours!" he exclaimed passionately.

"Someday, I'll set up organic farming methods in my village. I'm running short of finances, currently, but not short of faith! My loan application is pending in the village's co-operative bank. The moment I get it, I'll start with it! Until then, I'm surviving! Let's hope for the best."

"Let's shake hands, my friend; we sail in the same boat," Raghav greeted him with a smile.

"Give me two days. I will try my best to find away. God also helps those who help others!"

"I forgot to ask your name," Raghav said curiously.

"You are Prasad, right?" Lucky replied hastily.

"How do you know that?" Prasad asked with surprise.

"We have some observation skills, too," Lucky smiled, adding, "It's on your identity card."

They all smiled and headed in respective directions.

Chapter 16

The destination is seldom in sight! More often than not, it's not visible clearly! What reaches you there is the chosen direction. All you need to do is travel in the right direction. The destination then is only a matter of time.

As a routine, the housekeeping staff used to gather at nine in the morning for the distribution of daily tasks. Besides Angel's office, the main lobby and other two offices on the premises were also maintained by Taskforce Integrated, the housekeeping agency that Prasad worked for. The group had earned a good reputation among corporate clients in a very short period. Their approach was systematic, with regular staff training, and SOPs, such as, the daily task distribution meetings. Every individual at work was given clear guidelines on their roles and responsibilities.

Prasad, today, volunteered to take up the cleaning of the office cabins. The supervisor, although surprised, agreed. On any other day, he would have to plead to someone to get this job done. The task was risky, making a few people leave this job in the past, for not living up to the standards of the finicky, decision-makers of the company. But, Prasad had an exact opposite plan! He desperately wanted to get noticed by someone, even if it cost him his job!

The work was tedious and boring. But he had to do it in the best possible manner. It is said that you should find the work you love, for you to give your best. But that doesn't come true for the majority of people! However, the rest of the majority shouldn't feel like children of a lesser god. Albeit not entirely, one can always find something interesting in whatever work that has come up to them. It's not the work, but your involvement in it, that derives the satisfaction.

Prasad started cleaning diligently. Scrubbing every corner of the cabin one by one, he wiped the glass doors, cabin partitions, and door handles, apart from arranging files, and stationery. Some seniors were too busy to notice. Some offered advice every five minutes. But none were cordial enough to talk. By lunch, he had cleaned up three cabins. He had a quick bite, and started with the fourth cabin. The name on the door read Mr. Sudhir Acharya.

"May I come in, sir?" he asked, knocking on the door.

"Who's this?"

Prasad peeped in, "It's housekeeping, sir."

"Clean as fast as possible," Mr. Acharya replied without looking at him. He was deeply engrossed in his work. Shaking his legs and fidgeting with his beard, he was nervous. Prasad started cleaning the glass door and the partition, followed by the back credenza. A variety of files, all in different colors and sizes, occupied every inch of the credenza top. The only common thing Prasad could figure out, amongst them was the file title. This is what he was looking for! His eyes opened wide, reading the title. The common title read "The Feasibility Report of Start-up XXXX YYY ZZZ."

This was his 'Eureka' moment! No, 'Sanjeevani' moment! Because this task of finding the right person, was as difficult, as finding the 'Sanjeevani *Booti*' (herb) that Lord Hanuman had found from the dense forest of the Dronagiri mountain range.

Discovering a physical equation, seating in a bathtub, he thought, was much simpler.

Prasad's eyes lit up. The stage was set. The curtains were about to rise, and he needed to be ready for the act. However, nothing was scripted. He had to perform impromptu.

"May I put these files in order, sir?" he asked with caution.

"Hmm," Mr. Acharya replied.

"The dust suggests that this must be lying here for a long time," he said, trying to divert Mr. Acharya's attention. The result, although, was the same.

"Hmm," the reply was standard.

He was still looking for words, but just then, someone entered the cabin. Mr. Acharya was up to his chair instantly.

"Hi Sudhir, What's the progress on the new project?" the sense of authority echoed through each word.

"Rohit, I am going through proposals. I've also shared a couple of great ones with you. The online portal selling handicrafts looks promising."

Prasad didn't take long to realize the man was Rohit Mahajan, CEO of Angels. He was amazed by his simplicity and politeness.

"No more online businesses, please" his guidelines were clear. "The investors are ready with funds in hand. They could have easily gone to any other PEs. The reason they are choosing Angel's is only because of our ability to choose a radical, unconventional venture with a multi-bagger potential." he added.

"I understand. I am trying my best," Sudhir replied in a meek voice. Adding, "Please give me some more time."

"I am afraid, that's the only thing I can't afford to give you. The countdown has begun. You know what I mean. We have a lot of pressure," Rohit said this after he left the cabin.

The message was loud and clear.

Sudhir slumped in his chair. Putting his arms on his forehead, he cluelessly stared at the computer screen. He didn't even understand when Prasad left the cabin and returned carrying something in his hand.

"Sir, would you like to have a coffee?" Prasad brought him back to reality.

"Hmm, no," Sudhir said, trying to gather himself.

"Sir, if you don't mind, may I suggest something?" Prasad asked, drawing each card carefully.

"What?" Sudhir was still in his thoughts.

Prasad kept a file on his desk. "This is a start-up proposal. It's unique. This may meet your requirements." he said.

Sudhir looked at the file, sarcastically asking, "And you think, you know better than me?"

"Sir, I know that I don't know, and that's the only thing one requires to know." Prasad exclaimed, adding, "But that's not significant. What's significant is that if an idea can change millions of lives; generate employment for millions of naive, Indians, then it must be a great idea! And, that's what the proposal is all about."

Sudhir was dumbstruck by what Prasad said. Everything was too quick to digest. "I'll get back to you," was all he could say.

Prasad thanked him and swiftly moved out of the cabin. The bullet he had fired in the dark, had hit the target. For confirmation, he had to wait until dawn.

Chapter 17

The supervisor was tense the next morning. He grabbed Prasad, the moment he entered the morning meeting.

"What did you do yesterday?" he asked, anxious.

"What happened?" Prasad asked back, smiling mischievously.

"Mr. Acharya was looking for you. He wants to meet you immediately. Is everything fine?"

"I don't think I've done anything wrong," Prasad said, building up the suspense.

"Please go fast."

Prasad rushed like the wind to Sudhir's cabin.

"Hi, come in," Sudhir said, greeting Prasad with a big smile.

"The proposal looks exciting. I forwarded it to our CEO last evening, and surprisingly, he responded by midnight. He wants to meet them," Sudhir said, fully charged up. "So when can we meet them?" Sudhir asked

"Whenever you want, sir. They have been trying to meet you for almost a month, sitting in the lobby, waiting for a miracle to happen," Prasad's replied as he took Sudhir by surprise.

"Strange! God waits for you with his arms wide open. It's only the ego that creates a barrier," Sudhir replied philosophically, adding, "It takes some divine intervention for the communion. Call them immediately."

"There is good news," Prasad told Raghav and Lucky with a big smile.

Raghav and Lucky both were up on their feet, anxious.

"My business loan is sanctioned," Prasad said, adding, "I am ready for the take-off."

"Oh, that's... Good" Lucky didn't know how to react.

"Congratulations," Raghav tried to behave normally, adding, "At least you will reach your destination."

Prasad was enjoying his act.

"My dear friends, if things go right, we will all reach our destinations, sooner or later. And trust me, I won't leave you till you reach your destination too. Now quickly rush to Angel's. Mr. Sudhir Acharya is waiting for you. You are giving a presentation to the CEO." Prasad said, taking them by surprise

The board room was impressive. The glass façade that stood as the wall on one side, witnessed the growing skyline of Mumbai every day. The other walls were decorated in a mixed pattern of veneer and leather paneling. A giant screen rolled down from the ceiling for the presentation. The veneer clad, oval conference table, was surrounded by around twenty chairs, fully occupied today. Raghav and Lucky could see some familiar faces, staring at them with an intimidating gaze, like that of a professional boxer welcoming an amateur in the ring. The game was about to begin.

The murmur in the room was silenced by Rohit's entry. Everyone got up from the chair. He waved at them to sit down while settling himself right at the end of the table, opposite the screen. His sharp eyes winked, recognizing them from a distance. His cherubic smile, unidentical to his preeminent position, gave them a much-needed boost before the presentation.

The slides were few and concise. Raghav swiftly took them through the entire business plan, starting with the dearth of technical manpower, lack of accessibility by a real customer, the need for technological platform bridging the gap, further generating employment, data analysis of current implementation and future growth statistics. Ending the presentation with a thank-you note, he opened the session for questions and answers.

"Mr. Raghav, don't you think, you are proposing some kind of manpower supply agency?" the first question was like a punch straight on the face.

"You are right, sir," Lucky interrupted, continuing, "Only if you limit your vision to the current data gathered from a small suburb. What we are looking at is a nationwide application! Considering an average unemployment rate of five percent, we strive to serve close to seventy million people in our country. Moreover, you need to add an equal number of freelance technicians. Their contribution to the country is surely going to be far more valuable than any other manpower agency."

The score was leveled.

"Tell me one good reason, why should we invest in your start-up when heaps of ideas are biting the dust inside our storage?" a question flew to their faces, starting round two.

Raghav took the lead on this one. "Sir, I am sure there are plenty of ideas available. But I'll share mine. People replicate any successful model, with slight tweaking. If someone starts with female clothing online, the other comes out with female ethnic wear, the third one queues up with traditional wear, and so on. There is nothing wrong with this, except for the fact that you are going to get only a small pie in this saturated market. On the other side, if you look at our case, there is surely no guarantee of success. But, if we succeed, we'll have the whole cake served to us on a platter with the first-mover advantage."

The questions that followed were just raised to make their presence felt in the meeting.

"What kind of staff strength are you looking at?"

"What's the projected growth rate?"

"What's the estimated break-even period?"

Their confidence kept rising with an increasing number of questions. A sense of achievement started creeping in, irrespective of the outcome of the meeting.

"I have only two questions," all faces turned to Mr. Mahajan as he spoke.

"All ideas have a life cycle. Growth, Consolidation, and Decline. Do you have a 'stage two' plan? Do you foresee any value addition?"

Everyone was all ears.

"My second question is more technical. The success of an app is largely attributed to its innovative and affable user interface. And for that, you ought to have the best person in charge of coding. Have you narrowed down your choice?" Mr. Mahajan asked

Their answers needed to be precise.

"Sir, we do have a plan for the next level. To be honest, the idea arose just a few days ago, while waiting in the lobby. There is this guy named Prasad, who does the housekeeping in your office. And if, today, we have the opportunity to have this meeting, is only because of his efforts," he said, smiling at Mr. Acharya.

"He is an ordinary man with big dreams in his eyes, wanting to start his own business. But the lack of finance is distancing him from his dreams. For now, we are catering to only individual technicians and workers. But there are many like him with a goal in sight, but a hole in their pocket. When on the next level, we will cater to the requirements of such small entrepreneurs and connect them with the right resources. And, it may sound a bit out of context, but with your permission, could we, please have him here."

"Absolutely," Mr. Mahajan said, signaling to his assistant.

"Thank you, sir," Raghav said, adding, "As for your second question, our colleague and third partner, Ms. Jhanvi, has developed this entire app. She is currently based in Chennai on her work-based assignment."

"How can you manage such a big development with part-time help? It's not feasible" One of the members jumped on the opportunity to criticize.

Without waiting for any clarification, Mr. Mahajan interrupted with his final verdict.

"Raghav, Lucky, listen. I am in for the app, but with one condition. As far as possible, whoever has been developing it so far, should take it further. But it will be a full-time job. She should be able to quit her job, and of course, be ready to work at a lower salary till the break-even. Or else, hire someone else. I leave it for you to choose."

They both looked at each other. Their happiness was followed by a jolt of thunderstorms.

"Sir, there is no one by the name of Prasad in housekeeping. He is their supervisor," the assistant entered with the supervisor.

"What? We met him just before coming here. He was the one who referred us to Mr. Acharya," a surprised Lucky said

The supervisor stood confused, trying to remember something.

"Oh, wait, yes! I am sorry. That was Anjaneya. His name is Anjaneya Prasad. It's too long, so everyone just calls him Prasad. He just left work saying his job here is done."

Raghav and Lucky were shocked beyond words. Lord Hanuman is also known as Anjaneya, son of Anjani.

Chapter 18

"Jhanvi, join the video call fast!" Raghav couldn't control his excitement. They were still in the reception lobby.

"Why? What happened? Is all well? Give me two minutes" By now, Jhanvi had developed an inimitable sense of listening to all that was not spoken in words, by Raghav.

From the board room, the meeting had now shifted to the reception.

"We just finished our presentation at Angel's. And, guess what? They have agreed to invest in our idea. We are now ready to take off!!"

"Yes!" Jhanvi shouted ecstatically, nonchalant of the fact that everyone was looking at her in the cafeteria. "This is the moment we were waiting for! The road looks clear now! Get ready for an exciting ride." she kept talking.

"Everything is great, except for one thing. The road is still not made of roses." Lucky interrupted.

"Now, what?" Jhanvi dreaded at the thought of a problem.

Raghav was trying to find the right words.

"They are insisting on having a full-time coding manager. You are surely the first preference, but the compensation they can offer is much lower than the current one. We'll have to follow a very stringent budget till break-even," Raghav articulated himself.

"Oh!" Jhanvi absorbed the shock quickly. "Personal interests cannot conflict the company's interests. For now, I can't shrug off my commitments. So, it is simple. Hire a full-time coding manager. I am always there for any backup support."

Life's calculations are weird! As weird as the home loan EMIs! The small happiness of the principal quotient, comes with a huge interest cost!

Chapter 19

The show must go on! Angel's had given them an aggressive target of making their office fully operational within the next thirty days. They were pressed to work out the micro-planning. A small space, in a nearby industrial area, used for additional storage by Angel's, was made available to them. The place was small, yet cozy with a large corridor in front, leading to other such offices and a few industrial galas. Although, not a prominent address, the place meant something to them, and was very close to their hearts. It was their office!

The renovation was on at a breakneck pace. Modular furniture was essentially ready to be installed. Few linear workstations, a couple of cubicles, and a small conference room, utilizing optimum space were planned. Five of the engineering students from Classic Computers were also willing to join them immediately. Their dream was finally seeing the daylight.

Lucky smiled with satisfaction, looking at the work progress. They were in a comfortable position to inaugurate the office as per their target.

"Finally, everything is coming together!" he exclaimed.

"Everything?" for once, Raghav was not shying away from his feelings.

"You do get everything, except what you thought was everything for you!" his expression was loud and clear.

"Amidst all the hustle and bustle, I forgot to discuss this with you," Lucky said, trying to divert the conversation.

"Do you see any link here?" he asked.

"The person, coming to our rescue every time, bears a name similar to Lord Hanuman's. The first one was the actor playing Hanuman in a *Ram-Leela*, the second was MS, Maruti Nanadan Shukla, and the last being Prasad...Anjaneya..." Lucky added.

"Even I am a bit bewildered!" Raghav said, much to Lucky's satisfaction, adding, "It's a conflict within me. I don't know what to believe. Rationale demands evidence. Faith has its own conviction. Rationale restricts, but faith leaps in quantum. The heart, beats to a tune that the mind doesn't listen to. Whatever may it be, I do believe, signals of divine frequency exist around us. We just need to tune our antenna to the frequency of faith to receive it."

"You are right!" Lucky nodded.

"The inauguration is just a week away." Lucky said, getting the conversation back to normal, adding, and said, "Let's wrap things as quickly as possible."

Angel's had a tradition of organizing a *pooja* on the inauguration, on account of every fresh start-up. It was a low key affair to seek the blessings of Lord Ganesha, the God of good fortune. This was followed by dinner with friends and family. Lucky had informed his parents to come, and Raghav did too. But the one person, he was going to miss most, was Jhanvi. He blushed at his desire to possess a magic wand with which he could bring her there. By nature, he was too simple to think insanely, even in dreams. But, without insanity, love is more of a ritual than religion!

The day had arrived. With minimalistic decor and contemporary design, it was difficult to think of it as the same storage space, now transformed into a well-designed office space. The smell of fresh paint was lifted by the cool breeze blowing out of the newly fitted air conditioners. The bright LEDs lit up the space like a theatre. Garlands, made up of fresh marigold, adorned the entrance.

Dressed traditionally, Raghav and Lucky stood at the entrance welcoming guests. One by one, all the key members of Angel's started arriving. Formal greetings and courtesies slowly turned into loud laughter and friendly banters. Some headed straight to their single-minded target of delicious starters and fruit punch, while some, especially the women, were busy pouting, and making weird faces for selfies. Lucky's parents smiled and tried striking a conversation with Raghav's parents. Both hailed from diametrically opposite sections of the society, sharing one common feeling – the pride they felt for their sons.

A child is said to be born twice. First, when the parents announce their birth to the world. The second is when the world applauds their achievement.

Their parents were enjoying the second, and the more satisfying part of parenthood together. Raghav and Lucky mingled around with the guests, personally attending to everyone, being the perfect hosts. However, all waited for the one person, Mr.

Mahajan, to grace the occasion. Raghav was still looking for and longing for Jhanvi, who, surprisingly, hadn't called even once today, despite being well aware of the function.

Mr. Mahajan arrived at 6.30 PM, after finishing his final meeting at the office. He looked as fresh as he did at the beginning of the day, mixing around, cracking jokes, and laughing like a child. He then approached their parents and bowed down to seek their blessings.

The priest was ready with his preparation for the *pooja*, waiting for a nod from Mr. Mahajan. He signaled them to wait for five more minutes, and took Raghav and Lucky to a corner.

"How's everything going?" he asked.

"Yes, everything's fine, and in place." Lucky replied.

"I am talking about the office set up, not the catering service. When are the staff members joining?" he was back to business.

"Oh, five of them are starting from tomorrow. The others will join one by one in the next ten days or so," Raghav replied.

"My biggest worry is your coding manager. I don't think you've sorted that out," Rohit affirmed.

"Yes. We are working on it… We'll try harder." Lucky put up a lame response.

A good leader is also a good reader of what is said between the lines. The pauses in between "we'll try" and "we'll work it out" don't usually work.

"I had made clear the requirement for a full-time coding manager. He or she had to be on board even before the staff. Have you narrowed down on names? Do you think they will join in tomorrow?"

By this time, everyone had caught the attention of the serious talks among the three. Raghav and Lucky stood in silence, staring at the floor. They wish Jhanvi could answer on their behalf.

"Yes, sir. I am joining from today itself."

All eyes turned in the direction of the voice. A charming young lady, clad in a bright yellow sari, stood at the door.

Raghav could not believe his eyes. Lucky needed to pinch him to believe it. It was Jhanvi, entering in style, with her enchanting smile. She looked gorgeous and elegant in her never-seen traditional avatar.

"Good evening, Sir! I am Jhanvi. I have developed the product, and assure you a much-improved one in the future."

"Yaaayy!" Lucky screamed at the top of his voice, without bothering about the gathering.

Raghav stood speechless, as his eyes spoke for him. He could barely manage to keep his eyes dry.

"How did it happen?" Lucky questioned on Raghav's behalf.

"Well, I had put in my papers the day Angels approved you," she clarified, adding, "But, I couldn't ditch Syntel's. I needed a month to wrap up my work there and hand it over. So, here I am now! But at least tell me the name of our company."

"We were waiting for you! With Lucky, you and I, working in unison, let's call it Trinity!" Raghav replied

"Great!" Lucky gave a thumb up.

"But, how will you manage your financial issues?" Raghav asked.

"Don't ask me such difficult questions on the first day!" Jhanvi laughed, adding, "I'll have to part with some of my savings kept for the wedding. We'll opt for a registered marriage. Is that okay, Raghav?!!"

Raghav winked at her and laughed, saying, "My parents are here. Let's take their blessings and start the *pooja*."

The chants of the priest echoed in the office.

"*Vakrtund Mahakay Surykoti Samaprabha,*

Nirvighnam Kurume Dev Sarv Karyesu Sarvda"

Chapter 20

It was almost a year now. Time traveled at the speed of light. The business had gained good momentum. They were well on target, launching their services in one major city every month. 'Change is the only thing constant' was their fixed *mantra*. System upgrades were a continuous process based on user feedback. A dedicated team was carefully analyzing every feedback, even if trivial. The most important key to the success of any entrepreneurship is to honor customer feedback and quickly align with their requirements.

The delegation of duties was another important factor. Jhanvi headed technical operations, while Lucky looked into finance and marketing. Raghav was busy with the new launches, customer feedback, and management changes.

Angel's had established various systems of monitoring ventures. Weekly meetings addressed more tactical issues, while monthly meetings focused on strategic calls, cash flows, and other critical issues. This was in full attendance with top executives, including Mr. Mahajan himself. The meeting went on from morning till late evening with some serious debates and brainstorming. The crucial part was always the review of planned and achieved targets of the previous month, and establishing new ones for the upcoming month.

It was after one such tiring meeting, when Rohit asked Raghav and the team to come into his cabin. The cabin was the size of a conference room, with a separate cabin for his assistant outside. The decor was simple, with all white walls, except for the one at the back, highlighting a deep blue texture, creating a captivating contrast. The desk was clean with only two files, a MacBook, and a striking cool family photo frame.

"I guess, things are not too far off from the targets. Few unexpected roadblocks are inevitable," he said, rolling up his sleeves, loosening his tie, and relaxing in his high-back chair. Raghav, Lucky, and Jhanvi occupied their seats.

"The reason I called you here is different," he said, leaning forward." There is something big coming up."

All paid close attention.

"Post demonetization, the government wants to curb the use of black money, but a lot still needs to be accomplished. The government wants to minimize cash transactions, right from day to day transactions, to major dealings. They had come up with a bold vision of digitalizing the entire financial system. Currently, online transactions, credit cards, and UPIs are reasonably contributing to the cause. But, the spread is still limited to the educated, urban population. What the government yearns for is a universal, user-friendly system that can be used with equal ease across each tier of society. The one which covers the entire spectrum of transactions, leaving no stone unturned," Rohit said.

"Sounds interesting," Lucky responded.

"I have already taken the expression of interest in your name. The RFP (Request for Proposal) will follow, in the next week. The interested companies will have to submit their bid in two parts. The first one will be the concept stage, where everyone shall propose their idea, and solution with a brief execution plan. Whoever is shortlisted here, will go for the final presentation to the Finance Minister, himself. The one with the best value addition, optimum budget, shortest timeline, and above all, most stringent security features will be awarded the biggest IT job in the country," Rohit added.

"The vision is great. But, so will be the companies competing. The idea is exciting but intimidating at the same time. Don't you feel we're comparatively too small and unequipped?" Raghav said, realistically assessing the situation.

"Companies are never big. Your dreams are!" Rohit spoke with full awareness, adding, "Seeds of vision, nurtured by perseverance, turn into a full-grown tree of an enterprise. These big companies conducting multi-million businesses, are just like trains running on rails. A well-devised rail system does achieve efficiencies, but at the same time, stereotypes, and unidirectional thinking become detrimental for their growth and expansion. All decision-makers try and select the safest option, not keeping in mind the company's vision but their own self-interests.

No innovative ideas can originate from such a system. The idea for a project like this requires a flight of fancy, gliding high on strong wings of dreams. It ought to have a fearless vision, looking beyond the boundaries of the known horizon. And I can see that in your team! This is my belief in you! Now, it's up to you, in terms of, how much you believe in yourselves!" Rohit affirmed.

"Sir, your belief in us has led us to where we are today. We can't promise the best results, but we certainly promise our best efforts." Jhanvi said, leading the team's response.

"Okay. My assistant will mail you the synopsis of the proposal. Go through it carefully, and get ready with your primary idea when we meet in a week." Rohit said, concluding the meeting.

There was silence. Nobody uttered a single word walking out of the office, and getting the cab. The faith entrusted in them engrossed their mind completely. The responsibility was enormous, and so big was the need for a promising reciprocation, that nobody slept that night.

Chapter 21

They arrived at the office before everyone. The small conference room was the preferred place for all brainstorming. Brainstorming is a very effective management technique when it comes to any critical decisions, or generating new ideas. It works more like the ancient tale of a group of blind-folded people, trying to figure out an elephant. Someone thinks the legs are pillars. Some call the long teeth, a spear, while others think the tail was a rope. Everyone knows something, but in bits and pieces. When you join these pieces, and connect the dots, the truth unravels.

"Let's first define the problem," Lucky started, continuing, "Half of the solution is derived from knowing the problem at hand."

"Let's prepare the list of every transaction mechanism in the hierarchy of its evolution," Raghav responded.

"Cash comes first. Followed by cheque, net banking, then come cards, and the latest one, being UPI interfaces. Look, I am so intelligent." Jhanvi said, giggling.

"Okay, so what are its pros and cons?" Raghav fueled the discussion.

"Cash is always handy, easy to use, but the biggest problem is that it can go unaccounted," Jhanvi answered prudently.

"Cheque is a safe financial instrument. But it involves lengthy, cumbersome transactions, changing hands from the payer, to bank, to payee's bank account, and finally in payee's hand, if needed." Lucky replied.

"Coming to new age instruments, the cards, net banking, UPI's, etc., are certainly the most evolved and most efficient systems so far. But there is one drawback. It's more convenient for the urban population, which is more tech-savvy, attuned to technology. Hence, it has still not reached rural areas, compelling them to use cash." Jhanvi, answered.

"So, let's reframe our problem with more clarity. We need to merge the best of both worlds, to look for a new transaction instrument which is efficient and yet more simple," Raghav summarized the discussion.

"Don't you feel life's exams are cruel?" Lucky smiled, adding, "No marks for the steps. Either you pass by a hundred percent, or fail with a big zero! No in-between. Can we ask God to change this, please?"

Everybody started laughing. They didn't realize, the office was fully occupied by the time they came out of the conference room. The routine work needed equal attention. However, approaches for both, were poles apart. The routine work was more like a guided tour, with fairly predefined problems and solutions. While generating new ideas, it was more like an excursion in an unknown territory, charting new paths with the danger of getting lost at one end, and the excitement of finding a new road, being the other extreme.

Each day, each hour, each minute was crucial. Everyone was trying hard to crack the code. All possible alternates were tried out. Conducting meetings, researching, seeking expert advice, all was tried, but no insights. Ideas are like butterflies. You can't catch them, however hard you run after them. But when you sit quietly, expecting nothing, it slowly settles on your shoulder.

The discussions went on for long hours, sometimes lunch was missed, and sometimes dinner was managed in the office. Today was no different. The exhausting day, was put to rest, by a restless night.

"Let's break for tea," Lucky was visibly irritated.

"Should I ask the office boy to prepare your favorite masala *chai*?" Jhanvi asked, pressing the buzzer.

"No. Let's go outside. The tea stall at the street corner makes good tea." he replied.

"Good idea. We'll get to walk too," Raghav said, getting up from his seat.

With no breeze around, the atmosphere was gloomy. The dim street-lights made the road appear darker. The tea stall, however, was still busy with few people enjoying a hot cup of tea.

"*Bhaiya*, three cutting *chai*, please," Lucky ordered.

"Jhanvi, please proceed to go home," Raghav looked at Jhanvi, adding, "It's already late, and we still have one day to go."

"Don't worry about me. Few sleepless nights are okay if we are working out something for 1.3 billion people." Jhanvi replied

"What about you, Lucky? You also look tired," Raghav turned to Lucky.

"Oh. I am kind of an insomniac, and can't sleep. A cup of tea is sufficient enough to charge my battery," he replied, inhaling the aroma of the boiling tea.

"Your *chai*, sir," the vendor served them.

"How much for this?" Lucky asked.

"You forget this every time, sir. Its eighteen rupees for three," he said, smiling at them.

"There is some pending amount form the last time, too, I guess," Lucky said

"Yes, thirty rupees," he smiled again.

"How do you keep account of all this?" Raghav asked curiously, continuing, "Do you maintain a record book?"

"No, sir. I am an illiterate man, *angutha chaap*," he said, laughing. "But, by god's grace, everything is on the tip of my finger."

"Are you sure you can keep all the records on your fingertips? Amazing!" Raghav praised genuinely.

"Sir, that's the problem with this generation. It believes in machines, more than humans. Forget about God. He is last on their priority list! They need proof of everything. Tomorrow, even if God comes face to face, they'll ask for his Aadhar card, too!" he laughed, adding, "My son is of your age. He keeps asking me all sorts of questions. Once, he asked for the proof, of Hanumanji lifting the entire Dronagiri Mountain and all its medicinal herbs, on his fingertip," he said, pointing out to the tattoo of Hanumanji lifting the mountain.

Raghav, Jhanvi, Lucky were all ears now.

"Fact verification is for history books. Lessons learned from anecdotes are more significant to the present and future. By doubting, you limit the power of your own possibilities. Only a few hundred years ago, if somebody would have announced their plan to land on the moon, he would be called a lunatic. But today, it's a scientific achievement that everyone is proud of.

And forget it, if you don't want to believe this. But you can't deny the fact that all these humans, super-humans whom we worship as gods, across religions, have one common, implementable trait—their indomitable spirit of life. Not crying, but trying to overcome all the mountainous obstacles!" the vendor concluded.

This wisdom worked like magic for them. The butterfly had set on their shoulder, flaunting its magnificent colors.

"Let's go to the office. I am getting some ideas," Raghav said, finishing his tea and started moving without waiting.

"I'll settle the account tomorrow," Lucky said to the tea vendor and rushed behind Raghav and Jhanvi.

The office was almost empty, barring a few, like the sales guys and the office boy. They settled in the conference room.

Chapter 22

"What's the most unique, but common identity you carry with yourself?" Raghav started by asking.

"The cards?" Lucky said, scratching his head.

"No, nothing external to your body."

"You face?" Jhanvi replied, trying to read Raghav's face.

"Almost there…", Raghav said excitedly, continuing, "It's your fingerprint, guys! Remember, the tea vendor said, 'everything at your fingertip'?"

"Oh, yes!", Lucky said, banged the conference table.

"Now, if we link all the existing channels of transactions, to a fingerprint, our job is done," Raghav was figuring out more details.

"Can you please elaborate?" Jhanvi asked.

"Let's go back to the defined problem. What we needed, was to merge the efficient transaction channel, to the easiest identity option. What I mean is the current transaction system stays as it is, but the identity checks happen with fingerprints for daily transactions. No need to carry cards, and no computer interfaces are required! All the bank accounts of a person will be linked to his or her fingerprints. And then transactions can take place through fingerprints.

For instance, if we have to pay the tea vendor, we can just press our finger on his machine, and pay the required amount. That's equally applicable to a farmer residing in a far-off village. No need to carry any cash or card."

"So you're saying, every vendor will have to buy a POS terminal, like the one used for cards?" Lucky put the first brake.

"That's quite a number. But it can be thought of as a one-time cost."

"How about utilizing a smartphone?" Jhanvi came up with a better solution, continuing, "Most smartphones today have a fingerprint scanner. The same can be linked to a payment gateway. No need for a POS terminal."

"Wow! That is fantastic!" Raghav exclaimed as he sensed that they are getting some direction.

"Need to work out something for the ones without smartphones, who use basic phones. I'll include it in our target," Jhanvi added.

"Besides financial transactions, I guess the idea can also work for countless other applications!" Lucky said, moving back and forth in the conference room, adding, "How about merging all our essential documents with one identity? Remember, the tea fellow saying something like 'all records at your fingertips'…"

"Please elaborate."

"See, in a lifetime, one accumulates many documents, starting with birth certificates, educational certificates, property documents, medical records, statutory details, and so on. These are all printed physically, mostly kept unorganized. And one never knows when you will require which record. Thus, if we can digitalize all of these, and store them in a central repository, which is linked to fingerprints, then life will be so easy. For instance, a doctor can access my entire medical history just at fingertips, I mean, with fingerprints. The government can scrutinize all records linked to one person, simply at a fingertip! My educational records, and every single thing, all available at a fingertip! No verification is required by the employer. The possibilities are limitless."

"That's astounding, Lucky! Only you can come up with such an idea!" Raghav exclaimed ecstatically.

"No, not me. It's the *chaiwala*, who gave us the idea. We must thank him tomorrow."

"Let's leave. It's already late. We have to prepare the entire presentation tomorrow."

Chapter 23

The next day was hectic, as expected. They locked themselves in the conference room, strictly warning everyone not to disturb unless there's an emergency. Their approach to the presentation was simple, and not too flashy or colorful. The content was crisp, concise, and self-explanatory. The thought was always from the audience's perspective. 'What possible queries can they ask?' 'What possible doubts can they find?' And then try and incorporate the most logical, workable answers in the presentation itself.

By the time they finished, it was late in the evening. They were tired but satisfied. The joy of achievement glowed on their faces. It was time for a small celebration.

"Let celebrate in our own style with a cup of tea!" Jhanvi suggested.

"Oh, yes! I also need to pay the balance amount to the *chaiwala*." Lucky replied.

"We also owe him some royalty for the idea!" Raghav exclaimed, smiling.

"Oh, my god. We didn't ask for his name. I bet it must be on Hanumanji's name," Lucky said, adding, "Today, we can certainly catch hold of him."

They packed their bags and headed to the tea stall. The late evening breeze, calm and serene, played like soft music, while the neon street lights danced with the shadows. The road was clear, except with a few pedestrians. At times like these, the atmosphere tends to echo your mood.

They stood a little confused upon reaching the corner. The footpath was completely empty! There were no stalls there. The entire stretch of the footpath was clean as a slate.

"Where have all these stalls vanished?" Lucky inquired at the nearby shop.

"There was a municipality raid today. They removed all of them."

They looked at each other baffled, and in complete disbelief. Lucky just sat down on the footpath, with Raghav gasping in amazement and Jhanvi, going speechless.

History was repeating! Every time, when the clouds of darkness blinded them with oblivion, a tiny little star, far from the gloomy sky, illuminated their path, enlightening their life. But, when the time came for them to bow their heads, and raise their hands in gratitude, it disappeared mysteriously without a trace.

Chapter 24

"This is it!" Mr. Mahajan said, banging his desk in exhilaration.

Jhanvi had just finished their presentation in his cabin, with Raghav and Lucky anxiously waiting for his response. Every last drop of doubt about the concept evaporated with this reaction.

"I knew that only you could come up with such an out-of-the-box solution. 'The world at your fingertips!' what a great concept! Keeping all the financial transactions at your fingertips is undoubtedly a great idea, but more imperative is the convergence of all official details about all citizens on fingerprints. That is going to be our dark horse, the real match-winner.

We cannot undermine the fact that today, the best brains of the industry are vying for this project. All fiercely competing, to outsmart others. The differentiating factor will only be the value addition. It's going to be the prime parameter for selection.

And mind you, Syntel is also desperate to grab this job. 'Get it, or get out!' their CEO, Lokesh Raman, has received a final ultimatum by the management. Who else than you know at what level can he can stoop to save his neck!" Mr. Mahajan added.

All of them could visualize the real-time scenario at Syntel.

Chapter 25

The meeting room was more anxious than excited. The faces looking at each other were more scared than stimulated. The atmosphere was tense. The small whispers got dispelled by the entry of Mr. Raman.

A shrewd professional, infamous for his erratic temper, Raman probably held the record for sacking the maximum number of employees in the industry. His expertise was confined to achieving only two major goals. Increasing his net worth, and increasing the company's profit, in that order. The ways and means had no values. The end goal was the only justification.

He never mingled with the staff, nor met anyone without a prior appointment. But today was a different day, a difficult situation. He ought to address it before it slips out of hands.

 "Before we start the proceedings, let me remind you, that you are the most fortunate guys in this organization," he said, moving behind every chair slowly, akin to a beast hunting the prey, continuing, "You've bagged the privilege which none of those outsiders can imagine in their wildest dreams. So, picture this! I am the CEO of this company. I am the one who will guide you, interact with you practically every day! Isn't that great?! Look at me." He said with pride, continuing, "Your own destiny is at your disposal. Don't you agree, Ms. Suparna?" He stopped at a young lady wearing dark lipstick, with fake attention.

"Yes, sir!" She said, hurriedly keeping her mobile on the desk, adding, "You are one hundred percent right, sir."

"Good!" He said, grinning with a big smile, continuing, "What is your take, Mr. V. Bhushan?"

He turned his head to a short, lanky man sitting on the opposite side.

"Sir, the project is interesting but challenging. What I think is…"

"Now, you are thinking…that you can think too. Haha!" Raman said, interrupting Bhushan.

Everyone had no choice, but to laugh at the lame joke.

"If you all think that you could come up with great ideas, you probably would have been in my position," Raman said, chuckling.

"Don't stress your minds, just in case you have any. Only follow what I say. I already have a mind-blowing idea. You just have to follow it!" He said, staring at everyone with a squeezed eye, continuing, "The matter is simple. All we need to do is link all bank details of any person to one single ID. It can either be a universal card or maybe, their 'Aadhar' Card. He or she just has to make all transactions with a single card. Now tell me, what are your thoughts on this, Mr. Bhushan?"

"It's a great idea, sir. But may I add something?" he said, trying to be as diplomatic as possible.

Raman tried hard to conceal his annoyance.

"The use of cards is more popular amongst the urban population. We should also try and address requirements of the larger population, including those residing in rural areas, with no formal education." Bhushan added.

"What's your age, Mr. V. Bhushan?" Raman asked sarcastically, stressing the alphabet 'V.'

"I am thirty-three, sir."

"No," Raman shouted, continuing, "You are understating your age. You are a hundred and thirty-three years old, belonging to the 19th century. We are a progressive country. Each house has a television and is connected to the internet. Everyone is part of a global village. You better surf the internet properly!" he said, turning to everyone, continuing, "Listen to me carefully. I am not here to take any advice. My advice to you is very loud and clear. You are either bagging this project, or you'll find yourself begging for a job. Is that clear to all?"

"Yes, sir!" all responded in chorus.

Chapter 26

The bugle had called. The battlefield had heated up. All had braced themselves up, working hard, with sleepless nights to meet the deadline. The proposal was required to be submitted in the prescribed format, under strict protocol. A single, minuscule mistake, and the entire proposal would be disqualified.

All in all, twenty-seven proposals were received. Three of them got rejected for non-compliance. A committee comprising selected industry veterans, IAS officers, headed by the Finance Minister Mr. Shyamsunder, was entrusted to carry out the righteous, unbiased evaluation of each proposal and narrow down on the three best proposals for the Prime Minister's review. It was going to be a month-long exercise, full of in-depth reviews, intense scrutiny, and intellectual debates, trying to figure out the best possible solution for the country. An exhaustive balanced scoreboard, based on predefined criteria, was devised for an equitable evaluation. The task was herculean, with a critical impact on the future of the nation.

On the other end, everyone waited anxiously for the results, like it was their college final year results. All possible efforts were made and dusted. The papers were now in the hands of examiners. They had practically no choice but to prepare themselves for every possible outcome. This enforced helplessness compels you to a divine submission. There is nothing more you can do except completely surrendering to nature.

The day had finally arrived! All chaotic scrutiny and uncertainty had culminated in three best possibilities!

Chapter 27

"I knew it!" Raman said, moving frantically in the meeting room, adding, "I knew we would win this project. And that's what it has turned out to be!"

The pride of a winner oozed out from his body language.

"This is a tight slap on all those who raised doubts on my capabilities. I can only pity them. It's not their fault. Not everyone has an appetite for great things in life!"

The bandwagon started banging the table, in a chorus, "Congratulations, sir!"

"Sorry to interrupt, sir," Bhushan said, "But, there are two more companies also in the final race," he added.

"Mr. V. Bhushan!" Raman's face turned red, as he continued, "Sometimes, I wonder, if the company has hired you to advocate for others? Consider yourself lucky today. I don't want to spoil my mood by sacking you! But remember, I have terrible mood swings, and I am not apologetic!"

"Just for the record, the two companies you are talking about are nowhere near us. Vibgyor is known for its security lapses, and, what's the other company's name?" he said, scratching his head, "Trinity... yes! Those are the same kids, I'd sacked a few years ago. I can crush them anytime with my left finger."

The mood at Trinity was a complete contrast. The responsibility outweighed the feeling of victory. The excitement of selection was yet to arrive.

"At this moment, I don't want to sound pessimistic..." Raghav said sombrely, adding, "but, aren't we just small kids in front of Syntel and Vibgyor?"

"Kids are cautious while treading a new path. Chances of adults getting lost, owing to their overconfidence, are more," Rohit stated as a mentor.

"If God has got us up to here, he'll surely take us through this!" Jhanvi pressed his arm with a confident smile.

"Oye, why are you losing heart?" Lucky asked in full swagger, adding, "I am going to show Syntels, the blunder they've committed by laying you off."

"Let's not get personal, Lucky. We are not fighting against anyone. We can only compete with ourselves. The aim is not to belittle any organization. Our goal is much larger, much wider. We wish that with our contribution, we can make our nation proud, and be proud of the pride in turn." Raghav said, stating his code of conduct.

"Times up, guys," Mr. Mahajan took control, adding, "No more discussions, please. You have a horde of tasks to complete. The real game has just begun. Dive deep into all aspects. Try and find out as many loose ends as possible. Fasten them. Keep the FAQs ready for reference. We can send those in advance. This will solve many queries of the panel before the meeting."

Jhanvi noted every point down on her laptop.

"If possible, make a small-sized demo program. Check it for all vulnerabilities. Data security is going to be the prime deciding factor," Mr. Mahajan added.

"Nothing to worry about, sir. I am confident regarding this part!" Jhanvi responded, adding, "We do have a systematic testing mechanism in place. We keep an internal check of our own data against possible security lapses. In fact, we've got an internal group called 'Trouble Maker', that is constantly searching for loopholes in the system and attacking them. While the 'Trouble Shooter,' Tony Savio is a one-man army! A young prodigy, he has always outsmarted them on every front."

"Great! Then what are you waiting for? Let's get going, guys!" Mr. Mahajan said.

Chapter 28

The stage was set. It was much bigger than they could've imagined. From a street play, the performance was headed toward a magnum opus. They had to put all their acts together. Just the thought of presenting an innovative, integrated financial process to none other than the Honourable Finance Minister of the country, was good enough to send shivers down their spines.

The next few days were crucial. The entire office worked round the clock with their distinct deliverables. One group was busy making a demo program under Jhanvi's guidance. Lucky was looking at the FAQ preparations with other groups. Raghav worked hard on preparing the process flow, making presentations simple and concise. However, the most important aspect was data vulnerability. After all, they were working on a national financial system. A single loophole was enough to collapse the system, like a pack of cards.

The team of 'trouble Maker' closely scrutinized every aspect of the process flow, trying to figure out possible loopholes. This was first reviewed internally and subsequently posed as a challenge to the 'Trouble Shooter.'

The name 'Trouble Shooter' was a true synonym to the initials of Tony Savio-TS. From professional problems, to other personal issues, he had become the most sought after person in his brief stint at the office. Be it a problem in terms of proposing to someone, to the disposal of your old bike; he had a solution for everything. A state-level champion in chess, he was an avid marathon runner with an athletic body. He joined Trinity immediately after graduation to gain some work experience. His admission into a US University was confirmed a few days ago. The visa was the only formality left, and it was just a matter of time before he flew to the US for his Masters.

He worked well, as an ethical hacker, trying to identify the bugs and fixing them with patches.

COVID-19 was temporary, but its impact on everyday life was permanent. It's hard to digest that it requires negativity to compel positive changes in life. Bitter pills bring good health! For once, people had started opting for a healthier lifestyle. The environment was getting its overdue respect. The technology was becoming more people savvy.

Most meetings, nowadays, were taking place on online platforms. The one-to-one meetings were still not out of fashion, but online meetings were catching up with the race, at a tortoise's pace. The huge saving in time was the biggest advantage in addition to the cost savings. The proactive government had made it mandatory to conduct all meetings online, unless, otherwise, necessary.

The review meeting was to start sharp at 10 AM. The entire Trinity team was in the office right from eight in the morning. The technical team verified the virtual conference set up, while the presentation team was busy checking every slide. Jhanvi was preparing herself to make the presentation, rehearsing her vocabulary. Lucky, as usual, was parading across the corridor, biting his nails. Raghav occupied a chair in the corner, sitting silently in a meditative state. Mr. Mahajan arrived in, half-an-hour early.

"Hope everything is set, guys!" he was as inspiring as a football coach, adding, "Guys, it's the game of your life. All of you have done a wonderful job. Now, it's time to keep all worries aside, and just enjoy the show. Give it your best shot. If you win, everyone should smile. But god forbid, if you lose, make sure, your competitor has tears in their eyes. In either case, I owe y'all a party. Let the celebration begin! All the best, guys!"

The anxiety of the room turned into excitement. Everyone got charged up. The VC was just about to begin.

The Finance minister, Mr. Shyamsunder, welcomed everyone. He was a man of few words. Each word coming from him was like a *mantra*. Crisp, concise, and meaningful.

"It gives me great pleasure to welcome you all to this conclave for an integrated financial system. History is not just made up of stories from the past. It is very much created in the present by ignited minds like you, influencing the entire future, and I am here for the sole purpose of witnessing the future in the making. So, let's start the proceedings."

The Syntels were first to present. Mr. Raman, dressed to the occasion, in his blue Armani suit, started his presentation with his company's background.

"It gives me immense pleasure to welcome you all for this historic conclave as rightly pointed out by our honorable Finance Minister. Ours is a glorious history of becoming one of the fastest fortune 500 companies within five years of its inception. Needless to say, none of the companies out here are anywhere close to this landmark. We are currently operating in thirty-three countries with 65% clientele from the United States and the European Union, with close to ten thousand employees. I head the entire south Asia region comprising thirteen countries.

I am sure the company credentials will be the prime criteria when it comes to entrusting such a huge responsibility. The ponies are best for a country ride, but for winning derbies, an Arabian horse is the only option! Nevertheless, as a formality, I'll quickly take you through our proposal. I feel proud to utilize my twenty-five years of experience to this national cause. The unique idea developed by me is called 'One nation, One Card!' Currently, we use a variety of cards for financial transactions. I suggest merging all of them into one card, which is easy to handle and monitor. The rest of the proposition remains as it is—no need to modify any present system. Although everything is self-explanatory, I now keep it open for your feedback and questions. Thank you."

The Syntels' started clapping in self-admiration. The Trinity had already started sinking in the aura that Mr. Raman created. No matter, how hard you've worked in nets, the pressure of the finals against the current world champions, in front of half a million cheering crowd, is bound to weaken the strongest of the souls. All of them were dumbstruck.

"You are winning, guys," Mr. Mahajan said in a low voice with a sparkle in his eyes, adding, "Just wait for the questions, dear."

"Mr. Raman, can you explain where's the 'uniqueness' quotient in keeping three, four cards versus one card. Do you consider it to be a historical idea?" the questions were blunt.

"Sir, my wallet's size will reduce by half," Mr. Raman said as a few panelists laughed at him, while he thought they were laughing at his sense of humor, continuing, "On a serious note, all transactions happening through one card will greatly reduce the burden on back-end data. The cost of data centers will come down to half, with common servers. I can submit a detailed report if you wish. More so, tracking each transaction will be extremely easy. Bhushan, ensure that the report is submitted before next week," he added, turning to Bhushan.

"Yes, sir."

"Do you see any value addition in this?" another question was ready.

"Sir, I have devised this system purely and absolutely for upgrading the financial transaction system only. I don't like fusion food!"

"But the nation doesn't work on your likes and dislikes, right? Tell me one thing, do you think, a farmer working in a remote village, or a daily wage worker, or say some retired person, will be able to use cards with equal ease as the urban, young population?"

"Yes, sir. Even the illiterates of today are more tech-savvy than you and I. I don't see any challenge in this. Anyone who is still not conversant must be primitive," Raman said with conviction.

"My dear friend, my father, is a farmer, and is still active at the age of seventy-six. But he still prefers using his basic mobile. And yes, I do consider him intelligent for the fact, that most of his monsoon predictions are far more accurate than any satellite images. The project requires a universal appeal. You need to step out of your office and understand the ground reality" the blow was directly on the face. Raman had no option but to blush with a red face.

"Sir, your point is duly noted. I'll certainly work this out, and come up with a proper solution within a week."

"Let's not forget one of the most critical factors. Adopting this option requires minimal changes in the current structure. The integration would be seamless, saving a lot of time and energy," Mr. Kiran Madulkar, the principal secretary to Mr. Shyamsunder, voiced his opinion for the first time.

The man in his late forties has been the Finance Minister's trusted lieutenant, right from his earlier days of civil services. Mr. Shyamsunder had no hesitation in acknowledging his views in public when it came to making critical decisions.

"You said it right, sir! I conclude my presentation on this positive note. Good day everyone!" Raman said, ending his presentation.

For long, a stoic silence prevailed in the Syntel meeting room. The responses were far from encouraging, with the only saving grace coming from the principal secretary. No one could talk to each other, so everyone looked down and out. Bhushan looked at Mr. Raman's blank face. His eyes conveying the message, 'Sir, things could have been different, only if you'd have considered my inputs!'

"Please share your presentation, Ms. Jhanvi," the coordinator instructed. Trinities were the next.

Jhanvi adjusted her microphone. Dressed up in a traditional yellow *kurti*, and her hair neatly tied up, she brightened up the screen with her cherubic smile. No makeup, and no-frills. Nor was she dressed for the occasion. But there still was something enchanting about her! What matters the most is, what is within! Just like their presentation. The content was king. To be more precise, for Jhanvi, the content was queen.

"Good morning, Hon. Finance Minister and all the dignitaries. We feel honored to be participating in this historic meeting. Ours is a very small team, albeit, with big dreams. What we possess and what we're obsessed with, is the simple desire to make our nation proud, and be proud of it in turn. We surely cannot boast of the heritage Syntels harbors. But we do feel a strong connection with the glorious heritage of our country, inspiring the world for centuries.

Our project is aptly named 'World at your Fingertips.' If I may ask you, what is the most simple and most secure identity for any citizen? What would be your answer, please?" she asked, paused for a moment, continuing, "It's a no brainer. It's a person's fingerprints! Right? So if we can connect all the transactional instruments to one's fingertip, the job is done. No need to carry any card or cash. The whole world is at your fingertips!"

Raman looked up at the screen, squeezing his eyes, wondering to himself, "How could I not think of this?"

He quickly got up and tried sabotaging her presentation, before the idea could gain momentum.

"You think, you will replace all the current POS instruments? Did you have any idea of the costs of that implication?" he asked, desperately trying to destroy the idea.

"Sir, I was about to clarify this in the next slide. You can simply connect an add-on fingerprint reading device to these terminals. The one-time cost would not exceed more than 200 rupees," Jhanvi replied.

"Let's take a scenario if I go out to by some vegetables from a local market. And the vendor doesn't have a POS terminal. What do we do now?" the man who raised a query with Syntel earlier, got into the act again.

"That's the precise reason, why we've stuck to the time tested system of cards," Raman replied forcefully again.

"Sir, today almost everyone uses a smartphone with a fingerprint scanner. Taking its leverage, we've devised a connecting app that will complete further transactions," Jhanvi said.

"And what if I don't have a smartphone?" Raman questioned again, not allowing anyone to question.

"Sir, we have tried to answer this too" Jhanvi was now in full command. The initial inhibition faded faster, with each answer. She continued, "If you will please allow me, may I carry out a live demo? Hope someone has a basic handset around?"

"I have one," the coordinator nodded.

"Could you please pass on your number?"

The Syntels team, including Raman, were curiously glued to the screen.

"Let's say I need to pay you 100 Rupees. All I am doing is sending a message 100 <SPACE> your number" to my bank's dedicated transaction number. She pressed the send button and asked the coordinator to display his screen.

He flashed the message, 'INR 100 deposited to your account linked to this phone number.'

"That's amazing! What's the back-end working for this?" the Finance Minister, Mr. Shyamsunder, asked inquisitively.

"Sir, we have done nothing innovative. I just utilized the phone number linkage to a bank account. That's it!" Jhanvi answered, beaming with confidence.

"Great!" Mr. Shyamsunder exclaimed, visibly pleased.

"I reckon this has very much covered the financial spectrum" another person nodded, "But can it have wider application? I mean, is there any value addition to this?" he asked.

"Very much, sir."

Everyone, including Mr. Shyamsunder, to Mr. Raman, got into attention, as Jhanvi continued, "The benefits are much wider than they appear. For all the citizens, we propose to link every official record with their fingerprints. For example, if my university results are linked to my fingerprints, a verified copy is easily accessible to the HR department in a job interview. No verifications are necessary, and no worries about losing it by any chance. A patient can show their entire medical history to a doctor at fingertips! Imagine the amount of paper we are going to save. The environmental impact will be so huge. Your property papers, your assets, your vehicle details, whatever, you name it, and it will be available at the fingertips! And that's why we have named it 'World at your Fingertips'"

For the next few moments, there was pin-drop silence. Nobody gave any reaction, as they took their time to digest the idea. The Syntel's sensed the game was slipping out of their hands. The Trinity team thought they'd hit the bull's eye.

Mr. Shyamsunder broke the silence saying, "Your value addition seems superior to the core idea. Sometimes, sambar and chutneys are more delicious than the dosas, like my favorite hangout, 'Cafe Mysore' in your city. I have a very fond memory of the place from my college days."

"Sir, it's our favorite hangout too. Good to share something common with you!" Jhanvi said with a big smile.

"Don't you think this would enforce a huge system change collating all records under one roof?" Mr. Madulkar raised a valid query.

"Yes, it is, sir," Jhanvi said, explaining, "But, so was the case when we moved from ration card to election card, and now the Aadhar card. We can weigh the benefits versus difficulties before taking a call."

"Hmm," Mr. Madulkar responded, adding, "We need to take radical steps cautiously."

"Yes, sir! I leave it to the honorary members to decide what is appropriate for the nation, not just what appeals to individuals! Thank you so much!" Jhanvi concluded.

It was time for Vibgyors to show their spectrum.

The team was not as old as Syntel, or as young as Trinity. They'd bagged good projects in the financial sector in the last couple of years, but of late, faced backlashes due to a couple of security lapses. Somehow, they did patch it up in time.

"Good afternoon, everyone. I'll head straight to the presentation," their CEO Mahesh Nambiar led from the front.

"Ours is a completely different and radical proposal, different from any of the prevailing systems. We propose the complete elimination of the currency structure," he said, instantly noticing a few raised eyebrows, adding, "The currency system is an age-old system, and I am afraid, it cannot meet all the future requirements. We need to move to the solution of the millennium – 'Digital Currency.' People were visibly confused.

"The math is simple," he said, adding, "All current currency will be replaced by an equivalent amount of its digital form. A centralized ledger will maintain each and every transaction. These transactions can simply happen over cards, net banking, or any other means. This will not only ease out all the transactions but also provide complete transparency. No more cash, No more cheques, no more black money! The system is simple yet complex. I welcome all your queries now."

"This is by far the most radical proposal, and needs a lot of understanding," one of the officers initiated, adding, "The entire financial system can be at risk if there is a single loophole in the system. To me, it's too risky to even think of. At most, we can do some pilot projects and then gradually think of moving further."

"It is radical, but, very much practical, sir. For example, a few years back, all equity shares were in physical form. Now, everything is transferred to the dematerialized format. The system is not just running smoothly; it is operating at maximum efficiency."

"Some digital currencies do exist in the market, but they are too vulnerable," one of them raised their fear, adding, "There are so many instances of lapses. Frauds happen on an hourly basis. How do we guarantee a safer system?"

"Sir, we've done some analysis. The major reason behind this is the digital ledger, which maintains the data, is not under common control. While in our case, everything will be centralized with enough security measures."

"Do you believe people will adapt to this easily?"

"It's true that the new system would take time to settle in. But we'll have to negotiate the roughs for a smooth sailing future."

"Before we talk about the security of national data, let me share with you some local data," Raman was in his element again, adding, "Please answer with a simple yes or no. Three of your recent projects have serious issues in terms of data pilferage, leading to some serious frauds. Am I right?"

"But, the problem is fixed now."

"I simply asked you to say yes or no," Raman was getting under their skin now.

"Yes,"

"That's better. I don't think it needs any further explanation. Thank you."

The conference was coming to an end, as indistinct chatters took over the formal discussion.

"Good afternoon, everyone," the principal secretary brought everyone back to attention, adding, "Firstly, on behalf of our honorable Finance Minister, let me thank everyone for their wonderful participation. We have witnessed some path-breaking ideas today. This surely needs further evaluation. But one thing I am confident about is that the future of our country is surely in safe hands. The 'one country one card' idea does have some flaws, but will be easiest to implement. The 'world at your fingertips' appears innovative, while its implementation surely demands a lot of imagination. Digital currency is by far the most radical option requiring an equal level of diligence on its security aspects. The immense hard work exhibited by each team is worth the appreciation," he said, clapping, as it was echoed by loud applause, coming through every screen.

For a moment, it felt like all the three-teams won the coveted job; all the anxiety and hard work of so many months culminated in a sense of pride.

"And last, but not the least," he said, bringing everyone back to attention, "Your mammoth efforts demand equally diligent scrutiny from our end. We need time to carry out an honest, and unbiased evaluation of each proposal and be ready with our recommendation to the Hon. Prime Minister. Till then, keep your fingers crossed."

"All the best!"

Chapter 29

"Good show, guys!" Rohit congratulated everyone.

The mood at Trinity was jubilant. The stress and strain accumulated in the last few months erupted into loud cheers and high-fives. Some of them even started dancing. Amidst all the noise and voices, oblivious to the celebration, Raghav and Jhanvi were enjoying their quiet celebration of expressions. A relationship needs manifestation. Love is a festival by itself. Most relations cripple over the well-defined path of words. Love is limitless, flying high in the sky of eternity.

"It's time to celebrate, bro!"

If there was one person who understood their frequencies and enjoyed interrupting signals, it was Lucky.

Raghav smiled at being caught off guard.

"It's still a long way to go. We've seen things changing overnight."

"You are spot on, Raghav," blankly staring at the screen, Rohit corroborated, continuing, "Had it been any other person, I would have considered you as the winner right away. But you are up against the shrewdest, or to say without mincing any words, the most cunning person in the industry. I've known Raman from his early days. He is famous for his savagery, sacrificing careers of his juniors, and mentors, equally, when it came to saving his own."

They both could sense the tension in his voice, as he continued, "If my reading is right, he is not sitting in his office with his folded hands, praying for a favorable result. He must be planning something really dreadful!"

His prediction was as accurate as an astrologer's.

"Yes, I have a full-proof plan in place" Raman looked at the ceiling with his dreadful eyes, continuing, "You have a solution to every problem, sir" Suparna nodded her head as usual. Bhushan was visibly confused. Raman had called a meeting in his cabin with just the two of them.

"Bhushan, can you tell me, what type of person is Mr. Madulkar?" Raman's question confused Bhushan a bit more.

"I didn't get you, sir. Can you please elaborate?"

"You are dumb, as always. What I mean is, can he be influenced by any incentive? Money or otherwise?" he asked in a low tone.

"Sir, please don't even think on those lines. As far as I know, he is a thorough gentleman, with an untainted track record. On the contrary, if we go by the news lines, he has sacked so many corrupt officers," Bhushan said, almost pleading before him.

"So, we've got only one chance. And I am not going to miss this!" Raman said, adding, "Do one thing, take his appointment. I'll give you a bag of cash. You'll need to go to him and offer an entire sum for a favor."

By now, Suparna, who was completely indifferent to the conversation, got vigilant.

"That's pure *hara-kiri*," Bhushan said, shocked, adding, "Whoever is giving him the faintest hint of bribe is losing without saying. Whatever little chance we have, will be completely wiped off!"

"I am going to stick to this plan," Raman said, audaciously, adding, "Now listen carefully. Whatever I am going to tell you, will stay within the walls of this cabin. No one, other than three of us, knows this, am I clear?"

He closed the huge wooden door of his cabin. The closed-door secret took only a few minutes.

When the door was open, only Bhushan's voice was audible.

"Sir, please don't do this. This is not ethical."

"Ethics and values are meant for followers. Leaders create their own path, and I have the guts to prove it right, whether right or not. History is based on documents manipulated by winners, not on facts!" Raman proclaimed.

"Sir, please pardon me, But I can't be a part of this. My conscience doesn't permit me," Bhushan said, almost in tears.

"No problem," Raman stood indifferent in his expression. He could beat a chameleon in changing colors.

"I thought, this was your chance to get the promotion eluding you from so many years! Nevertheless, Suparna is intelligent enough not to miss this golden opportunity! Right, darling?" Raman added, smiling at her.

"Who me?" she was completely caught unaware. "Sir, do you think, I can perform this task?" she asked.

"My dear, only a jeweler knows the true value of a diamond."

"Is it?" she asked, not convinced, adding, "If you have so much faith in me, I can't let you down" the lamb was honored with the garland swinging around its neck.

"Bhushan, kindly excuse us," Raman said, looking at him, sarcastically, "We've some important points to discuss," he added.

Bhushan got up in haste and almost ran out of the cabin.

"Sir, don't you think, being aware of the plan, he is a big risk for us?" Uncanny to her usual self, Suparna was talking sense now.

"Don't worry, baby. I'll kick him out the day we bag the job. You accomplish your task, and pack your bags to work on international projects! I am ardently waiting for the day of the results! Syntel declared as the winning horse. I wish I could be there with the Trinity, to look at their defeated, dejected faces!"

The horse, like in a game of chess, is capable of performing some mysterious moves. It is the only piece that can move forward as well as backward in a random pattern. The most menacing part is, it can easily jump over the others! A quality not gifted to even the King!

Chapter 30

The faces at Trinity were anxious. It was 11.30 AM already. The elected winner was supposed to be intimated by 10 in the morning. The staff was in no mood to focus on daily tasks. Lucky moved frantically in the office corridor, while a visibly nervous Raghav tried finding solace in Jhanvi's eyes, which in turn could not conceal her anxiety. Mr. Mahajan was sweating, despite the chilled air-conditioned temperature.

Going by the presentation, they were pretty confident of qualifying. But going by experience, the result may swing like the Indian cricket team. Beating the best teams in league rounds and finally losing the finals! The uncertainty was getting unbearable.

"No point in waiting, Raghav. Please call and confirm," Rohit said.

"Okay, sir!"

Raghav dialed the number at the Ministry. Every heart in the office skipped a beat.

"Sir, this is Raghav from Trinity. I just wanted to inquire about our proposal."

No one moved an inch from their place.

"What? But, why? That's out of the question, sir! We don't stoop to such levels. There must be some misunderstanding. Sir, I request you…"

The phone got disconnected.

Raghav felt the entire office spinning around him. He could barely manage to stand on his feet, slumping into a nearby chair.

"What's the matter, Raghav?" Jhanvi asked worriedly, looking at him.

"How is this even possible?" He was still shocked.

"Just tell me, what did they say?" Lucky shouted.

"They said, we are disqualified on ethical grounds!"

"What?" the entire office echoed in shock

"They said someone from our office tried to bribe the principal secretary Mr. Madulkar. He didn't tolerate such nonsense and disqualified us."

Not a single person in the office could believe what they were hearing.

Now, I am getting it," Rohit tried to compose himself, asking further, "Who bagged the job?"

"It's Syntel, sir!"

"I knew this! I told you…" Rohit said furiously, adding, "Raman! That bastard can go to any length to protect himself!"

"But, how can he do this in our name?" Lucky wondered.

"I'll tell you how…" they heard a soft voice from the reception area. It was Bhushan standing at the reception.

"You have been working at Syntel for so many years, Mr. Bhushan. You must be happy today. Don't tell me, and you are here to share your joy!" Raghav reacted, upon seeing him.

"Just a small correction! I 'was' working with Syntel's till 10 o'clock, this morning" his face resonated with his grief, as he continued, "I was sacked with immediate effect the moment the result was announced. Mr. Raman is far more cunning than anyone could ever imagine."

"I'll kill that bastard," Lucky said, fuming with rage. "How could he do this?"

"The plan was simple. He sent Suparna, my colleague, disguised as a Trinity employee, trying to bribe the principal secretary."

"Holy crap!" Rohit was shocked and surprised, and added, "Only a bastard like him can do this."

"This is the irony of life that I was worried about. A cunning person gets rewarded for his cunningness, while an honest person pays the price for their honesty."

"But how did he create the identity of our employee?" Jhanvi asked.

"You still doubt his capabilities? Too naïve," Rohit replied.

"I feel helpless to the core! Never ever in my life, have I felt so bad about us", Raghav wept inconsolably.

"It's okay!" Jhanvi gathered herself, adding, "Together, we shall overcome this too!"

Jhanvi gently put her arms around Raghav's shoulder.

"The frustration is not about losing the job. But it is about our dignity and integrity that was attacked with such brutality, leaving us completely helpless. We just can't do anything" Raghav couldn't stop himself, continuing, "Today, the truth, once again, is left completely outsmarted by the malicious lie."

"We still can do something!"

All eyes turned in the direction of the voice. A black sleeve, with a silver bracelet, was waving at them from the far off corner.

"For smart problems, we need to work out smarter solutions. That's it!"

Although he was sitting with his back facing them, everyone recognized him in an instant. A completely contrasting character, he was surely in a different league, in all respects. On a typical weekday, when the entire office could be seen in formals, here he was, roaming around in a sweatshirt, swinging his trademark silver bracelet and humming songs.

He was none other than their own Trouble Shooter, Tony Savio.

"Dear Mr. Trouble shooter, just for your information, this is a real-life problem and not a program bug! I need to think twice," Lucky said, inviting him to the front.

"You get the game by your attitude, bro, not by thinking!" he exclaimed, giving a cool look.

"Okay, then show us the attitude, please," Lucky was losing it.

"Who is the guy from Syntel?"

"I am here," Bhushan raised his hand.

"Okay. So you were sacked today morning, right?"

Bhushan nodded his head, staring at the floor.

"All are requested to take their places, please," the startling authority in his voice made everyone obey his orders instantly.

"Let's move to the meeting room. Only the core team, please," he said, looking at Raghav.

It was only the six of them inside the room, now.

"Tell me your system ID and password at Syntel, quickly," he ordered Bhushan.

"But they must have deactivated it by now," Lucky reacted.

"No harm in taking a chance. The IT guys are normally busy with so many routine issues. I presume deactivation would be their last priority. I hope it works till the end of the day!"

Bhushan quickly surrendered the required details.

TS started weaving his net. His hands moved like a magician on the keyboard. Glaring at the screen with anxious looks, his mind was busy multi-tasking. Raghav, Lucky, Jhanvi, and Rohit, stared intently at the screen.

"Yes! Got it!" TS thumped the table. "We have access to their system, although a limited one," he added

"Wow! That's great!" they said in unison, as the computer screen reflected the silver lining on their faces.

"What's the name of the person, who tried to bribe in our name?"

"She is Suparna, Suprana Nakate!"

"So, what's the plan, TS?" Jhanvi asked, trying to decipher.

"I am trying to get to her official records. If we can manage to get substantial proof of her employment at Syntel, then we can turn the tables around! What say?"

"That's super cool, man," Jhanvi said excitedly, adding, "Let's pray to God. He will work out some solution."

"For now, I will try to work out something. So let's not bother God!" he said, smiled at them.

All kept their fingers crossed.

"Oh crap, no!" he said, raising his hands in the air.

"What's the matter?" Bhushan asked.

"I was trying to access the HR module using your ID, but couldn't go beyond a point. These details are accessible only through the employee ID JE6784. Date of joining, 27th May 2018."

"Yes. Correct," Bhushan confirmed. "What else do you need?"

"They can delete this in no time," TS said, adding," What we need is a copy of her employment letter, or a payslip, or salary account details which becomes self-explanatory of her employment with Syntel."

"Spot on, TS!" Rohit exclaimed, visibly elated at the idea.

"But, how do we get through this now? We are hitting a deadlock again," Raghav said, clueless.

The emotional roller coaster ride had left them high and dry. But it was still far from over, getting increasingly scary every moment.

"You said something about attitude. What can attitude do here, bro?" Lucky asked TS.

"The energy fuelling our thoughts, is a double-edged sword. If you panic, it turns into tension, but if you believe in yourself, it becomes a tonic. The choice is yours!"

"But what choice do we have now?" Lucky asked nervously.

"We have to barge into the bastion," TS said, getting up from his chair.

Everyone was now bowled over, unable to understand a word.

"I need to go to Syntel's office and get the physical copy of the document," he announced with stoic determination.

Everyone in the room thought they misheard it.

"Are you nuts?" Rohit asked in complete disbelief.

"Are you out of your mind?" Lucky added.

"Do you think you are talking sense?" Jhanvi asked, continuing, "Let's assume, you are successful in sneaking in the documents. But what if they find out about this, and lodge a criminal case against you?"

"Let me remind you that you are all set to fly to the US for your masters. You will be receiving your visa in a day or two. We can't risk your career for the sake of this project. It's not fair."

"And what Syntel did is fair?" he said, giving a sarcastic smile, adding, "Don't worry about me. It's time for Syntel to worry about themselves. We need to act fast, and we need to act now! Mr. Bhushan, I need a few details from you."

"Sure, tell me."

"Who is the HR executive looking after recruitments? Say for someone with similar experience as me."

"Shalini Sharma"

"Give me her number, please. I want to apply for a job at Syntel," he said, smiling.

Everyone in the room became increasingly anxious due to the suspense.

He dialed the number given by Bhushan and put the phone on speaker, indicating everyone to be silent.

Chapter 31

"Hi! Is this Shalini?"

"Yes, who is this?" The voice replied.

"I am Tony Savio. Congratulations! I heard you've bagged, probably the biggest IT project in India today. So, now that you must be looking to employ more people, I was wondering if I could be fortunate enough to get an opportunity to work with your organization."

"It will take some time. Things won't change overnight. Anyway, you can drop in your resume on my ID. We'll get in touch with you once a suitable position opens up. My ID is..."

"Ma'am, I've just mailed my resume to your ID. Request you to verify it, please," Tony said, interrupting her.

The voice paused for a moment.

"How do you know my ID? I am a bit surprised. Also, how do you know our company has bagged this project? We haven't made any official announcements, yet"

"There you are, Ma'am" TS was now weaving the net outside the internet, adding, "You are so intelligent! Let me get straight to the point, Ma'am. I am working for Trinity, your biggest competitor, for the project. Now you need to quickly rush to your CEO, Mr. Raman, and inform him that there are good chances of him losing the project," he said after a long pause.

"Hello? Are you there?" the voice on the other end got nervous.

"Yes. I can offer all the secrets, which is enough to place the final seal on the deal."

The voice was now serious. "Do one thing, come to our office tomorrow, in the afternoon."

TS began working faster than a computer processor. The other five in the room together could not match up with his speed. But they were more elated, than frustrated at their limitation.

"Now what?" a visibly worried Bhushan asked.

"Only you can save us, now!" TS said, laughing, adding, "You need to guide me with the HR recruitment process. Where do they conduct interviews, how long it takes, how far is the print out bay from there, and most importantly, where and how, do they store the physical copy of the employee database."

"That's something I can surely help you with. I was in the HR department, the entire morning. There are two cabins near the reception. The interview generally takes place in one of them. The department uses a common printer placed at the extreme corner near Mr. Martin's cabin. Also, about the records..." he stopped for a while. This morning's incident played a re-run in his mind, continuing, "The year-wise records are kept in the document stacks, right opposite the pantry. My resignation being the latest addition in it," he said, almost crying.

"I should get Suparna's document somewhere there, right?"

"Yes. Only if you're able to locate the May-2018 file!"

"I am all set, bro."

"TS, I know you've solved many technical bugs, and have the potential to be the best 'Trouble Shooter' in the industry, but today you are risking your entire career for us. I want to know why?" Jhanvi asked guiltily.

"I don't know. Even I am a bit surprised. But, there something within, urging me to follow this path." By now, TS looked cool and composed, adding, "I will let you know if I ever figure it out! But for now, forget the rest and hope for the best."

The meeting ended with a high-five.

Not much had changed at Syntel in terms of décor, except that the reception table was now moved to a corner, creating more space for the visitors' sofas. They were growing at double rate, compared to the increased number of people visiting their office.

Tony informed the receptionist about his details. As anticipated, Shalini came running to the reception. A young lady in her late twenties, looking dapper in her business suit, she walked up to Tony and hurriedly escorted him to one of the meeting rooms.

"Nice office, I must say," Tony said, mapping his observations. He was more a spy than an engineer today, carefully noting each door, corridors, work stations, etc.

"So Tony, you were saying something yesterday," Shalini started the conversation.

"Yes, I was telling you that everyone at Trinity is planning to sabotage your project."

He still wasn't looking at Shalini, and she was found it increasingly awkward. But it was time to focus on something more important. She was specifically instructed by Mr. Raman to extract details from Tony, and verify them before bringing him to his table.

"We've already received the confirmation. Are you saying that it can still get reversed? Interesting! Hmm!" She waited for him to react.

"I can provide you everything, as per your interest, but what about my interest? Have I been assured of a job here?"

"Call it a clichéd HR question, but I still have to ask!" she said, continuing, "Why you want to quit Trinity and join Syntel?"

"It's simple, ma'am. Whoever bags the biggest project of our country, will undoubtedly be the number one enterprise in India. And I don't settle for anything but the best in life!"

By HR standards, his arguments were crap. But, by situational standards, they sounded logical to Shalini.

"Your job and future, are secure with us. Rest assured. Our CEO, Mr. Raman, believes in long term relationships!"

TS gave her a disturbing smile.

"Ah! What about the details that you wanted to share with us?" she pretended to act normal.

"Oh, yes! Everything is in this pen drive. Would you like to take a look?" the spider activated its sleep mode, alluring insects to enter the web.

"The pen drive doesn't work on my PC. I need to take IT's help. Will you mind waiting for a while?"

"Oh, I am good. No problem," he said, getting ready for the adventure of his life, continuing, "Do you mind guiding me to the loo?"

"Go straight and take the first left. It's just opposite to the pantry."

"Great. Thanks!"

TS started his stopwatch. He had exactly ten minutes to accomplish his mission. He entered the loo in front of Shalini and came out instantly searching for the pantry. It didn't take him much time to locate the pantry, as he saw a couple of staff members hanging around, with a coffee mug. However, waiting for them to move out from there, really tested his nerves. He stared at his stopwatch, which ticked faster than the speed of light.

With only 5minutes and 36 seconds left, he quickly sneaked into the document control area, presuming no one has noticed him from behind. First things first, he needed to find the chronology, according to which the records were maintained. It required shuffling through multiple stacks, to establish the order. The next step was to search for the employment files for the year 2018. He prayed Shalini would remain busy taking his irrelevant printouts. The slides were deliberately unformatted, intending to buy him some more time.

Like that one sadistic professor, life draws pleasure in throwing those questions, you are not prepared for! He was about to experience this in the most critical test of his life!

Out there, Shalini was visibly confused, generating the unformatted prints. She assumed she was not too naive to fix this print issue, but, knowing Mr. Raman's temper, she didn't want to take a chance. She rushed to the reception, much earlier than TS had anticipated.

"Where's that guy?" she asked the receptionist.

"Who?" the receptionist took a while to recollect, continuing, "Oh, yeah, that guy. I thought he went inside with you!"

"He had gone to the loo. Has he not come back yet?" Shalini's confusion turned into anxiety now. Hastily, she rushed inside.

TS was about to grab the coveted trophy! His hands were gently reaching out to the file titled "Employment-MAY-2018" when a petrified voice shouted from behind.

"What the hell, are you doing here?" Shalini's expressions were louder than a horror movie scene.

TS was completely caught off guard. He was not prepared for the surprise, but there was nothing he could do, other than quickly adapt to the precarious risk.

"Oh, I forgot to tell you! I always wondered, just as you have the privilege of conducting our background verifications, why can't we have the liberty to verify the company's credentials, as well? Isn't it fair?"

He was as cool as an Air Force pilot, caught behind the enemy lines.

"I'm afraid, I don't get you."

"Rest assured. I'll ensure, you'll never be able to get me," he said, tearing off a record from the file, keeping it near his chest, adjusting his hands. Shalini couldn't figure out what he was doing.

"You can't do this!" Shalini became hysterical.

"The verification of your company states that you've tried to bribe the Finance Ministry of India by using your employee in Trinity's name. Your CEO's mistake will be paid through the nose by every employee," TS was talking nonchalantly.

"I'm calling the security" Shalini went nuts.

"That'll be the last nail in the coffin, Ma'am!" TS commanded with pride, like a prisoner of war, adding, "You better call your CEO. I have a very fair and final proposal for him. It's your last chance to save the company."

Shalini was completely blown off by now. Numb and indecisive, she just followed what TS was saying.

"Let me have the privilege of meeting the CEO, Mr. Raman," Tony emphasized on 'the,' quite boldly.

They headed straight to the right-end corner of the office. The area was an independent office-within-office, isolated from the rest, with a carved metal mesh. It had its own waiting area, a big meeting room, a restroom, and a small gymnasium as well.

Shalini didn't wait for the secretary's permission, and barged straight inside the cabin, instead. She came out as quickly as she went in, waving at TS to get in.

TS got up from his chair. He was confident, yet cautious. The person he was about to meet was responsible for ruining the careers of so many stalwarts of the industry. The time had now come to sabotage the career of this treacherous creature! If successful, he was sure of receiving a multitude of blessings from many innocent souls! This thought alone gave him a much-needed conviction.

The office was an opulent reflection of Raman's personality. Everything was larger than life here. His metal-clad desk was bigger than any board room table. The golden-hued curtains matched the sparkling gold chandelier. His favorite lounge chair was studded with sparkling crystals.

"Welcome, my friend" Raman was at his diplomatic best, behaving as he had just met an old friend in a coffee shop.

"Tell me your wish, and it will be granted!" Raman boasted, adding, "You are sitting with the most powerful person in this industry."

"That's nice to hear! You'll certainly require a lot of strength to execute my offer!"

"I can do it with my left hand. You just name it, and it will be done," Raman said, looking at the papers in TS' hands.

"Just a small request," TS took a long breath. Raman had his attention. TS continued, "All you have to do is to confess your wrongdoing to the Finance Minister, and give Trinity its rightful dues!"

"Are you out of your mind?" Raman changed in a flash, fierce and furious.

"You think, I am afraid of school kids like you and Raghav. I was the one who ruined his career a few years ago. Do you really think I was not aware of his credentials, potential, and contributions? It was just that I wanted to depute my confidence in his project! And so I sacked him! It's as simple as that!"

TS was stunned to hear this! His eyes, his face, and his whole existence turned red with anger. His hands became stiff, ready to slap him tight.

"You will see history repeat itself, even today. He is a born misfortune, accepting defeat in the name of virtues and principles. I don't believe in this nonsense. I create my own fortune," Raman's ego spoke for him, continuing, "When I first saw you, I thought you are an intelligent man, not a fool like him. You are here to create a fortune out of this situation, but you seem to be as dumb him. At this moment, you're the only person who knows the truth. The world will come to know if you walk out of this place with proof in your hands," he came close to TS, adding, "And you think, I'll let you go so easily? You've yet to see my real colors!"

"Security!" Raman's scream sent a shiver down the office.

A hefty man came rushing inside.

"Get this paper from this man's hand and throw him out of the office!"

"Oh, sir, I am so sorry. You misunderstood me. Pardon me. I was just trying to gauge this paper's value for you," TS was smart at playing chess, outwitting every single move of his most clever opponent.

Raman was perplexed, and not sure, how to react. The security personnel was in a dilemma, waiting for further instructions.

The moment had arrived! The pawn was ready with his final move! The King was exposed from all sides with a checkmate.

"Sorry for believing in me!" TS said, winking at him, adding, "Now you can't blame anyone, but your own self for the consequences," bypassing the security, he started his marathon, leaving everyone behind.

"Catch that monkey," Raman shouted. "He should not go out of the office," he added.

This was a unique marathon for TS. Marathon with hurdles as a work station, office corridors as field track, the steeplechase by security guards, and a relay document, he had to carry till the end. The one thing he was sure of was that 'he couldn't afford to lose this race.'

It was quite an unusual sight for a corporate office. A strange-looking guy was jumping from one workstation to another, banging every cabin door, bypassing the passages and corridors. The security guards were going crazy trying to nab him. The chaos all around was unimaginable! Nobody could figure out what was happening around them.

Finally, security was successful in cornering him. Two of them stood in front of TS, while one approached from behind. He looked around, up and down. There was no way he could escape now. He stopped where he was, breathing profusely, raising his hands. It was time to end the race.

"This is the paper that you are looking for, right" his eyes still fluttered, searching for something.

"Hand it over to us, and we'll not harm you," the security guard started inching towards him.

But, before anyone could realize, he grabbed a lighter from a nearby desk and burned the paper. The shock treatment, though, was far from over yet!

"Just listen to me carefully, guys," he said, getting everyone's attention. "Your CEO Mr. Raman has tried to bribe the Finance Ministry in our name. Unfortunately, you all will be the victims of his crime, and I can only feel sorry for that! The paper burning is my hand is not the proof I was running after. A scanned copy of the document has already been forwarded outside, through a small camera in my T-shirt button the moment I got it! I just wanted to give Mr. Raman, the taste of his own medicine. He is responsible for burning the entire fort with his selfish motive."

He glanced above in anticipation. The smoke had started entering the smoke detector housed on the ceiling. The floor's fire alarm started hooting tremors. The Public Address system began announcing an automated message.

"It's a fire. It's a fire! Please evacuate! Use the fire escape route."

The panic button was hit. Nobody could understand anything, and they were clearly running out of time. They started running towards the fire escape door.

"Fire! Fire!" the shouts filled the office air, as the security personnel ran for their safety.

TS took a carefree walk to the main corridor. He got down through the main staircase and vanished. The mission was accomplished!

Chapter 32

Any visitor coming into Trinity today, would be zapped upon seeing the scenes. The office had transformed into a party zone, with the sound of music playing through cell phones, at a limited output. The joy, flowing freely through the faces, was limitless.

You tend to witness some of the most hilarious acts during such impromptu events. Few demure characters suddenly start giving out rock star performances! Some bathroom singers turned into self-proclaimed opera singers, just not giving up the mic!

Bhushan witnessed mixed feelings. Lucky got into the groove with his unbeatable *bhangra* moves. He grabbed Raghav and Jhanvi, bringing them towards the center. Everyone circled them, cheering. They were both reluctant, Raghav being shyer among the two. Jhanvi took the lead, exhibiting her elegant dancing skills. Raghav followed her footsteps, but could manage only a few steps! The whole floor erupted.

The wait was long, but it was worth it all. Undoubtedly, they were happy over the win. But more than that, they were happy for the fact that they survived a very hostile character assassination. And everything was possible because of one person TS. The Trouble Shooter in the true sense!

It was more than three hours since they got the images from him. Bhushan also got feedback from his Syntel colleagues about his heroic escape and forced fire drill, evacuating the entire office. They were all getting worried about him, when Raghav's phone rang.

"Where the hell are you, TS?" Raghav tried concealing his anxiety, adding, "Hope everything fine at your end."

"Yes."

"What you've done is incredible, man! We owe you a treat! Rather, we owe you everything! We are indebted to you for life, my friend! All are waiting to see you. When are you coming?"

"Can you please put the phone on speaker?"

Raghav was puzzled. He put the phone on speaker mode. Everyone was waiting to hear his voice.

"Guys, I am not coming back!"

The party suddenly halted. The silence was deafening.

"What?" was said in unison. No one could believe what they'd just heard.

"You must be joking," Jhanvi was in denial. "Don't irritate me. Tell me where you are?"

"Listen, guys. Currently, I am in the waiting lounge of Chatrapati Shivaji International Airport, ready to fly to the US. To tell you the truth, my visa had arrived just before this issue cropped up yesterday. I had to attempt this mission today itself."

"And you want to leave without even meeting us. Didn't you feel like spending even a couple more days with us?" Lucky was visibly disappointed.

"Had it been a normal situation, I would have surely stayed for a couple of more days. My ticket was already booked for next week. But in case this mission would have failed, I would have landed up in police custody. Who knows, even today, if someone has lodged an FIR, I would be compelled to stay back until I am proven innocent. I needed to avoid these complications, and had no other option but to advance my ticket for today."

"This was too risky! Going behind the enemy lines, challenging them in their own territory, you executed the plan like some spy thriller!" Raghav was in awe, adding, "From where did you get such courage, my friend?"

"That's in my genes. My father, Squadron Leader Ashvin Savio, was a prisoner of war. He resumed his duty the day he was released by enemies."

"No wonder," Rohit reacted, continuing, "Both of you deserve a standing ovation."

The entire office stood up in attention; the sound of claps played like a beating retreat.

"I wish we could have celebrated this success together," Jhanvi said, sobbing.

"God willing, our paths will cross someday. Until then, have faith in yourself. Have faith in God. "

Every eye in the room was moist. Moist with a feeling of pride, and a feeling of joy. Every heart in the room, beat with the same beats, the beats of togetherness, of happiness!

Raghav, diverting his attention, stared at the emblem on a currency note. It read,

"Satya Mev Jayate."

Truth alone triumphs.

Chapter 33

The formalities that followed were subdued as compared to the high octane drama leading to this event. Raman was stripped of his honor with immediate effect. Syntel had to issue a public apology, dissociating them from Raman, saving their leftover grace.

The project was handed over to Trinity in a formal ceremony, from the hands of Honourable Finance Minister, Mr. Shyamsunder. The office had started running at a break-neck pace. However, the space was unable to match the pace. Shifting to a bigger, a better place was the need of the hour. They struck a good deal, with a ready-to-move-in office, almost three times the current area.

Performing *pooja* on any auspicious occasion had become more of an SOP at Trinity. It was a low key affair by their growth standard, with only staff and families having a nice, cozy get together. Everyone dressed up in traditional attire, having fun, enjoying the moment.

Raghav, Jhanvi, and Lucky were having an animated conversation in one group. Their parents, by now, pretty conversant with each other, had started enjoying each other's company.

Everything looked picture perfect. But something was still missing for Raghav. Looking lost halfway through conversations, he was in his own universe. Before Jhanvi, there was one person, who read his mind like an x-ray. It was his mother. Naive in other aspects, she was the most clever when it came to her son. She got up from her place and slowly reached out to Raghav and his company. Jhanvi shifted to her left, making space for her.

"From tomorrow, your son will sit in this grand office" Lucky held the water bottle like a microphone, enacting a TV journalist. "Now, tell me, ma'am, how do you feel at this moment?"

Everyone started laughing.

"We are happy to see all of you happy. The grandness is irrelevant" the life lesson was short and simple.

"Before me, you need to ask this question to your friend Raghav," she said, smiling, "Something still seems to be bothering him."

The revelation came as a relief to Jhanvi. She resonated with her with an instant thumbs up.

Raghav was cornered from both sides. A little amazed, he confessed his confusion in an instant.

"Yes, *Maa*. Something has been bothering me for a long time," Raghav said, adding, "and I am unable to decipher this mystery."

The group got curious, as Raghav continued, "You remember the ordeal we faced while I was expelled from Syntel?" his voice got heavy, as he continued, "We should never forget the time when we had nothing."

"Hmmm," Jhanvi concurred with the emotion.

"And you know? When I was on the brink of losing my last hope, someone appeared from nowhere, giving me the strength to move forward. Apparently, he was an actor essaying the role of Lord Hanuman in *Ram-Leela*."

He turned to Lucky, saying, "Can we forget the days when we had nothing in our pockets, and we were daydreaming about finding an office space and staff to establish our start-up?"

"Yes, bro," Lucky nodded his head in agreement

"And the manager that came to our rescue, Maruti Nandan Shukla, again bearing Hanumanji's name!"

And Jhanvi, don't you see any coincidence in the fact the idea of the project 'World at your Fingertips' was given by the tea vendor having Hanumanji's tattoo…"

"Hmm," Jhanvi nodded affirmatively.

"I still haven't got over the latest instance. This is no less than a miracle, when our Trouble Shooter friend saved us from the worst humiliation, while at the same time defeating the most powerful person in the industry. It's next to impossible!"

"But did you notice?" Lucky pointed out, adding, "There is an exception this time. His name is Trouble Shooter. I mean Tony Savio. None of Hanumanji's name"

"Yes!" Raghav said, adding, "But his act was as adventurous as the burning of Lanka by Hanumanji."

The group was astonished upon establishing the link.

"What was the name you mentioned just now?" *Maa* asked.

"Tony Savio"

"No, you said something else... Troubl..."

"Oh, that's his pet name. Trouble Shooter"

"What does that mean?" *Maa* couldn't understand.

Everyone was confused. Translation from one language to another is a very precarious matter. The literal translation tended to sound funny and obscure, losing its significance in translation. They had to try anyway.

"Trouble means 'problem.'"

"Oops, Hindi!"

"Trouble means..."

"Means 'Sankat'!"

"Bingo!"

Everyone tried hard to solve the quiz.

"How do you translate 'Shooter'?"

"*Nishana Lagane wala*. Haha."

"Shut up!"

"It's Sankat Mochan," Raghav shouted.

"It's SANKAT MOCHAN, Hanumanji's name again. The remover of obstacles!"

The crowd went hysterical, as the mood swung from confusion to chaos.

"*Maa*, now you are getting me? How can we consider every instance as a mere coincidence? The solution to each of our problems has only one common factor, none other than Hanumanji! Don't you think, this is a miracle?" Raghav was completely blown off, adding, "*Maa*, please guide me. I am so confused."

"Okay, let me tell you something!" Everyone settled themselves, as *Maa* continued, "Miracle, in general parlance, is receiving something without doing anything. A genie comes out of the bottle and fulfills all your wishes, whether you are worthy of it or not. Whether you deserve it or not. Or at the most, you may call it divine intervention."

"I am not getting it," Jhanvi said. "*Maa*, please elaborate?"

"I'll start from scratch."

"We want to hear."

"To comprehend this, you need to first understand the true essence of Ramayana."

Everyone flashed the first bencher look, confident of knowing the subject even before the teacher has started teaching.

"I know you know the Ramayana. Ramayana is an epic! Ramayana is a heritage! But your reference point essentially comes from the stories you've heard from your grandparents, the popular TV serial, or at the most, some reference reading. In a nutshell, it's the story of Lord Rama, that we've heard countless times, and we tend to believe we know everything. A story where Rama defeated Ravana. A story, celebrating the victory of good over evil. A story that dates back to a few thousand years. We are not even sure if the story still has any relevance in today's scenario. All we can do is admire Rama, worship Rama as Lord!"

"Yeah, but that's what the truth is"

"Yeah, that's what the truth is, but that's not the only truth! It's easy to visit the temple and worship him, but, it's difficult to follow him. It's easy to praise his deeds, but difficult to imbibe the virtues. God, at times, is just a religious escape for not performing our duty. We are mortals, weak souls. We can't reach close to him! So, instead of following his footsteps, it is easier to admire him, worship him and absolve ourselves from performing the rightful duties.

If you observe his life closely and neutrally, you will be amazed. The God that you pray to, for good fortune, the God that you pray to, for a worry-free life, has faced the most unfortunate, most painful events throughout his life.

At the tender age of thirteen-fourteen years, despite being a Prince, he was taken to the jungles by Rishi Vishwamitra to fight against the dreadful demons. The day, the entire city of Ayodhya was busy celebrating his coronation, he was sentenced to live in exile, for a long fourteen years! And that too not for any faults of his, but to keep his father's promise. Imagine his plight, when he couldn't even meet his beloved father at the time of his death. Leaving all the comforts of royal life, living a hermit life with his wife and brother, under constant threats of a frightful forest, were more than adequate reasons to shake up any human soul to the core. Making things worse, the ordeal stretched, when his wife was kidnapped by the Demon King. Searching her in deep jungles, without any direction, without any clue was an impossible challenge thrown at him by life.

The events of his life look glorified if you read it as a story. Put yourself in his situation, and you'll surely have sleepless nights. Life is a treacherous trader. At one moment, it gives you all the gumption and glory, and the next moment, it leaves you with nothing.

Every one of us goes through such a crisis at some point in life. The magnitude may vary. It is this moment of predicament, that pushes us to the crossroads, compelling us to choose a path. One approach leads to Ravana, who, despite having all the power and wealth in the world, set his evil eyes on someone else's wife, eventually sacrificing all his near and dear ones, destroying his entire empire.

And here is a person, who has willingly given up his kingdom for his loved ones. Despite being subjected to the ugliest miseries in life, he never for a moment, swayed from the eternal values and the principles of truth. The bitterness of events has only made him a better person, proclaiming unshakeable faith in life. And when one does this, life reciprocates with all its generosity. For him, the help came in the form of Hanumanji.

It is because of his faith that they could build a bridge across the sea, all the way to Lanka. And it is because of his unwavering courage, that he could defeat Ravana's mightiest military with the help of Sugriv's relatively untrained force. Calling it a miracle is only undermining the indomitable spirit of the human being. And trust me, this is a universal truth, applicable across religions. Names can vary; the truth remains constant.

Understanding religion, and understanding existence, is like measuring the limits of the sky by the size of your window. Different followers, peeping through different-sized windows, are fighting for ages, assuming the expanse of the sky by the size of their respective windows. Sitting inside the house, they are right from their perspectives. Yet, if you look beyond, all are wrong! Our mind is conditioned to think of what is comprehended to its limits. Existence is limitless, boundary-less, embracing everything, embracing everyone. But, you need to go beyond your window and embrace it equally. Do not try to measure it just immersing yourself in it!" *Maa* concluded.

Everyone in the room was stunned, unmoved, and completely immersed in the words of wisdom that flowed from a naive, uneducated lady.

"Coming back to your question, should we call the help that you received, a miracle, or a mere coincidence?

I don't wish to call this help a pure miracle. I rather consider it divine intervention. Life is full of surprises. Some days are good, and some days are really bad. The liveliness of life lies in its uncertainty, and unpredictability. Without it, it's just monotonous, and worthless. Misfortunes are external events, beyond our control. But facing it with a smile, keeping intact all the principle and moral values, is in our hands. It is your '*Karma*'! Throwing you into the depths of despair, is destiny's prerogative. Sailing through it, keeping your hopes alive, is your dignity. Puzzling you with an out of syllabus question is a life lesson, and facing the consequences with confidence is your answer. Even when all is lost, you can still do a lot. Just keep the humanity in you, alive, and I am sure life will reciprocate with its divinity. Existence loves you, cares for you much more than you can imagine! Someone from somewhere will surely come to your rescue and remove all your obstacles," *Maa* concluded.

Everyone got on to their feet and started cheering.

"Jai Shree Ram!

Jai Shree Hanuman!"

The divine sound filled each and every corner of the office, each and every corner of their hearts!

www.ingramcontent.com/pod-product-compliance
Lightning Source LLC
Chambersburg PA
CBHW070647220526
45466CB00001B/327